TAYLOR MONTGOMERY'S WALKING STICK

A North Alabama Family Memoir of Daniels,
Montgomerys, Barrons, Cooleys, and More

TAYLOR MONTGOMERY'S WALKING STICK

A North Alabama Family Memoir of Daniels,
Montgomerys, Barrons, Cooleys, and More

TONY DANIEL

**DARK
COFFEE
PRESS**

For those who are living in the family's present,
to offer a reminder of the past,
and encouragement for the future.

Author's Note

Here is an extended reminiscence whose theme is my family. I try to discern something of the personalities of my ancestors, along with the bare facts that I could uncover. It's not a history. I am not a professional historian. It does not purport to be a completely accurate genealogy backed up by immutable facts, because I'm not a professional genealogist. I'm a writer and editor by trade.

The book tries to stick closely to the facts and to put matters in historical context, but is, by no means, comprehensive. I could have dived into research on the coal mining industry in the mid-20th century, or farming practices in the 19th century, or the horrors of World War I, or the Spanish Flu, and so much else. But that is not where my interest lies in this book.

What interests me here are the personalities, what I can discern of my ancestors, as well as the facts. There's plenty of great history out there. My great-grandmother died from the Spanish Flu. There are books about its ravages in 1918-1920. My great-grandfather was hit by mustard gas in World War I. Much more can be discovered in far better researched tomes than I provide here. What none of those works contain, however, are accounts of my family members.

I have not attempted to keep my personal judgment out of this book. I have a lot of opinions about the relatives I grew up with and knew. I love them all, but I was not blind to their faults or to their virtues. I hope that I have portrayed them all as people, and not as caricatures. I tried my best.

I have some amazing ancestors that I know only a very few things about. I have Revolutionary America era ancestors. Men who fought. Women who endured and triumphed. All sorts of stories can still be discovered in the historic record and in the DNA. I've stopped with what I know is verifiable. I didn't want to present any wild guesses as established fact. Families have enough crazy stories that later turn out to be untrue, or gross exaggeration, or even sometimes the opposite of what is true. I don't want to create any of those fables here.

With that said, I must add that I have not included footnotes, a bibliography, an index, or any other accoutrements of historical research. The main reason I have not is because my sources are mundane and easily located. Aside from some unique family material I possess, everything is found online at genealogical web sites, military record sites, and newspaper archives. It just takes a bit of poking around. I may include sources and an index in a later edition, but, for now, this will have to do. Although this is a written work, I've tried to maintain the rough character of an oral account. I've mostly let repetition and colloquial expression stand.

This is all true as I can make it. The opinions are my own. It is a portrait of a river, a great river of memory and its tributaries, that lie in my imagination. What is a family, anyway? It's a waking dream, a mental conception that allows a person to be strengthened against the adverse tides of the present, or to deepen present contentment and happiness. In either case, I hope that my descendants find this dream, this slice of their own history, useful—and entertaining.

Tony Daniel
Wake Forest, North Carolina
July 2020

Contents

The Lost

Every branch of my family that I have discovered has, without exception, been in America since before the American Revolution. There are no nineteenth century immigrants. My wife, who is from Germany, will be the only twentieth century immigrant in my children's lines, and she came over in 1991. There are men who were Confederate soldiers during the American Civil War, but none for the Union. There are at least two American Revolutionary War vets, probably more. The Gunters, on my mother's side, seem to branch back, via the Robbinses, to Plymouth Colony, and perhaps even to the Mayflower voyage itself.

Almost all of them, men and women, were farmers, until the early twentieth century.

Many have been lost. About 199,800 years are unaccounted for. I suppose my people started out in Africa, some 200,000 years ago. It's pretty clear from the mitochondrial DNA that at least the women in my family all come from the same line. Somehow or another the ancestors I know about got up to Europe. From there, we came across the Atlantic. The DNA test says about seventy percent comes from England and Ireland. I am, as we Americans say, profoundly Scotch-Irish. Oddly, there is a double-digit percentage from Switzerland, specifically the Grison canton. No real idea where that comes from, but perhaps from the DePriests, who maybe hailed from France, or the Lances, who were definitely from Germany.

There are rumors in my blood of Native American heritage. The DNA test says point three percent (0.3 percent), but I've never seen any proof of it in the ancestors I know. People say my thrice great-grandmother Louvisa Barron was Black Dutch and looked like an Indian, but her Pritchett parents are pretty obviously Georgia settlers. Yet perhaps not. That would be Georgia Cherokee blood, then. My

1

DNA has about the same percentage of African origin. Again, no idea or indication where it came from.

Also, I have a significant number of Neandertal variants. Or so the experts claim.

Part 1
The Daniel Branch

The Daniels

The Daniels in Randolph County, Alabama, are part of a multi-generation record of church minutes from the Providence Baptist Church in Woodland, Alabama. I first read those minutes in the spring of 1991 on loan from my Aunt Ethel Daniel Mooney, while I was living in Randolph County, Alabama, for several months. Now that Aunt Ethel has died, I possess her copy and her transcription.

My grandfather's name is Emmett O'Neal Daniel. His father was George Francis Daniel, and his father was Isaac Elijah. The Woodland church minutes paint a nice picture of Elijah's father, Hartford Daniel. He was kicked out of the church for dancing. Then some time later, he was readmitted to the fold, and eventually ended up a deacon and officer of the church.

Hartford Moss Daniel (1839-1915)
and Elizabeth Williams Daniel (1842-1917)

Hart was a Civil War veteran, a soldier for the south. He served as a private, I believe, in Company B (which was apparently a cavalry company) of the Alabama Fifth Battalion, CSA. The battalion was known as Hilliard's Legion, also. He was captured August 27, 1863 in Jacksboro, Tennessee and, it seems, waited out the rest of the war as a prisoner at Rock Island Barracks camp in Illinois. Hartford Daniel is one of at least five Confederate veteran ancestors I have.

George Francis Daniel (1882-1974)
and Rior Jane Gore Daniel (1883-1969)

I knew my great-grandfather Daniel, George Francis. We called him Pa Daniel. I believed many called him G.F. He worked a farm in Randolph County on what became County Road 92. He eventually developed Alzheimer's or some such vagueness, and was put into a nursing home in Anniston, Alabama. The staff there was given to tying him up in his wheelchair. The family discovered this after George one day systematically dismantled the wheelchair with his fingers and escaped. He didn't get far, as he had very little idea of who he was at that point, but the nursing home was compelled to call the family, who looked into the matter. George was taken home, where I believe his son Robert, and my Aunt Ethel, looked after him. He died a couple of years later.

George had two sons and many daughters, five daughters in all. My Aunt Ethel is the youngest of his daughters. She is the one who showed me the copy of the Providence church minutes. The sons of George, Emmett and Robert, were never particularly close, I don't believe, and they persisted in a feud into their late 80s.

I was slightly acquainted with Uncle Robert. Robert lived near home his whole life, and eventually became a farmer on the partition he inherited when George died.

In fact, I was present at a family meeting when the division of G.F. Daniel's land was discussed. I saw an aerial photograph of the, I believe, 200-acre parcel along County Road 92. Division lines had been drawn for each piece to be apportioned. My grandfather opted for the least farmable, but prettiest section. This would also allow him to keep cows, as it had a creek. Robert took the most fertile, because he was a farmer.

Emmett developed a hobby farm on his parcel—which was, as mentioned, a much prettier portion of land. During the 1990s, the address became 8245 County Road 92, Newell, Alabama. To get to Emmett's parcel, one had to pass through Robert's land. As Robert got older and the Alzheimer's in both brothers made them loonier, tensions between the two escalated, with Robert threatening Emmett and my grandmother, Myrtice, with a gun on occasion.

I believe the basic problem was that Robert persisted in acting as if the whole place was his, and Emmett was there by permission. It isn't hard to understand why. Robert had never left the land of his father, except to go to war. Why should he now confine himself to a portion of it? Alzheimer's is no respecter of legal niceties.

Both put up plenty of barbed wire fence to mark their land, however. It seemed a silly feud to Ethel. As the brothers descended into dementia, the feud became likewise incomprehensible, but no less bitter.

Robert seemed crazy when I knew him, and Emmett was never a forbearing man. I suppose they died unreconciled.

In any case, I have only slight memories of their father, George Francis Daniel. Pa Daniel seemed very country to me, a boy who grew up in towns. He did not bother with flicking away flies, for instance, and it bothered me that they crawled on his clothing. Now I can understand the impulse. There is cow manure and corn everywhere. You get flies. You can spend a life shooing them, or ignore them.

Pa Daniel liked the swing on his farm house porch a great deal. I think that carried on throughout his life. There was no air conditioning, after all. He was in the midst of Alzheimer's decline when I knew him, of course.

His wife was loved by all, it's said. Rior Jane Gore—I think George called her Gallie, or Gal—is a broadfaced, friendly looking woman in photos. My mother liked her, and she did not like many Daniels (for good reason). My mother's childhood with my kindly maternal grandmother and great-grandmother did not prepare her for Emmett and Myrtice, who often were judgmental of others, it seemed to me, almost as a vocation.

Ethel Muriel Daniel Mooney (1921-2009)

I don't remember meeting any of George and Rior Jane Daniel's daughters other than Ethel, although I suppose I must have. My father liked his Aunts Pink and Becky, I recall. And everyone liked Ethel, the baby of the family. Ethel married an odd, but nice, fellow, Carson Mooney—a thin, lonesome looking fellow, but with good hair—and they never had any children. Ethel worked as a bookkeeper her whole life, I believe, and saved a great deal of money, which she put into Randolph County land, buying up clear-cut portions (that is, portions of land that had been pulpwooded) when they were for sale more cheaply. Over the years, the trees grew back, and the land value increased. Ethel was quite shrewd about this. When she died she bequeathed thousands of acres of ready-to-harvest pineland to her family, including my father.

After some legal wrangling with one of Uncle Robert's sons (whom I did meet a couple of times and was not impressed with), the whole lot (it was mostly timbered land) was sold together to a forestry company, and the money doled out according to Ethel's portions.

I believe that the inheritance from Ethel was the money my parents used to purchase their 2010 Toyota RAV4, the last automobile they possessed. It eventually came to me in an unbelievable state of disrepair. We eventually sold it for $1,300, and it served as a down payment for our present car. So in that sense, Aunt Ethel helped me out monetarily, which I believe she would have enjoyed knowing.

Isaac Beck Daniel (1814-1884)
and Elizabeth Lovvorn Daniel (1814-1880)

There are other Daniel names that echoed in my youth, such as Uncle Gabe, who was George's brother. George's great-grandfather Isaac, and his wife Elizabeth Lovvorn Daniel, were a force in the area. In the surviving photo, which may be authentic, he has a big, face-shrouding beard. As I mentioned, Isaac was an officer of Providence Church and often represented the church at area conclaves and such over many decades. It's all there in those church minutes. It's hard to get an idea of his personality from just those minutes, but my impression is that he was an outwardly stern, but inwardly kindly man, with a sense of humor (he is reported absent from a meeting of church officers once with the excuse that he "forgot it was Sunday.")

I sometimes wonder what happened with Hartford and that charge of "dancing," in the minutes which resulted in a suspended church membership. Was he dancing with his future wife, Elizabeth? What kind of war did he have? He was taken prisoner at what looks to be the beginning stage of Chickamauga. It must have been dreadful being a POW.

Isaac Elijah Daniel (1858-1936) and Susan Esther Dorrough Daniel (1855-1932)

Hart's son Isaac Elijah and his wife Susan Dorrough Daniel I have no clear idea about. I. E. Daniel was a farmer. Until my grandfather, who was an electrician and later a successful electrical contractor, all the Daniels were yeoman farmers, landowners living on the red clay soil of Randolph County that had to be worked hard to make pay.

Isaac and Susan must've both lived through the Civil War as youngsters, Susan slightly older, and Isaac with his father Hart away fighting. I suppose his mother, Elizabeth, was taking care of the kids by herself, or likely with the aid of relatives. I think Sherman's army passed east of Randolph County, however, as it swept down into Georgia from Chattanooga.

More Daniels

Isaac Beck Daniel's mother had the maiden name of Barsheba Beck (1770-1860), and Beck was Isaac's middle name. It is said the Daniel line continues back to Isaac's father, a possible Revolutionary War veteran from Tyrell, North Carolina, Aaron Daniel (Aaron was a junior, and lived 1762-1820, although the DAR currently disallows him as a Revolutionary, I understand), and beyond that to Aaron (the senior) and to a Thomas Daniel and his wife, Elizabeth Lanier (who may have come from Barbados) and two generations before that, Roger Daniel and Avis Bell, immigrants from Bristol, England. There traces are lost. I have seen no evidence that actually connects Isaac Beck to Aaron and Barsheba, however, only family trees. The evidence that "Beck" was Isaac's middle name is from two of his signatures on a widow's pension affidavit from 1892.

There was definitely a Bersheba Daniel. She's a bit of a legend in Randolph County. She was Isaac and Elizabeth Lovvorn's daughter. She cut quite a figure in the late 1800s. Bash Daniel (1841-1899) was said to have been an excellent business woman, even a bit of a loan shark, and, if the photos are truly of her, weirdly beautiful. She dressed sumptuously and had very good horses and buggies.

She's said to have paid a man, W.T. McDow, to marry her in the 1880s, to please her mother. She already had five children, but not by McDow. Their surnames were all Daniel, and all were born out of wedlock. It's not clear who the father(s) might have been. She was a lifelong churchgoer (although some seem to have been ashamed of her), and was said to sing beautifully. Anyway, her given name might well have come down from Barsheba Beck Daniel, if that woman was indeed Isaac's mother and Bash Daniel's grandmother.

Perhaps I will learn more with DNA and more digging around later. Isaac's mother Barsheba Beck's parents were a Founding Era couple, as well, and her father may have been a continental soldier. I seem to have several Revolutionary War veterans (and no loyalists, at least to speak of) on both sides of my family.

Emmett O'Neal Daniel (1912-2008)
and Myrtice Magdelene Boalt Daniel (1921-2012)

My paternal grandfather sometimes called himself E.O., but generally went by Emmett. I'm not entirely sure where the O'Neal came from, but the governor of Alabama at the time of Emmett's birth was Emmet O'Neal, who had advocated for rural credit unions and land banks, so I strongly suspect his parents named him after the governor (although somewhere along the way little Emmett picked up an extra "t" on the end of his name).

I always found Emmett a bit of an enigma. When he got older and developed fullblown Alzheimer's, he was erratically mean toward me as an adult. I didn't understand it at the time, because I didn't know what was happening to him.

Yet Emmett was never an easy fellow to get along with in the best of times. He didn't talk much to me over the years. I think I participated in his general disappointment in my father, whom he'd wanted to become a professional man, probably an electrical engineer. In the end my father did just fine as a cartographer at Hunt Oil and as an artist on his own, but this fate was seemingly beyond Emmett and Myrtice's vision.

I know they were either nonplussed or hostile toward the fact that I became a writer. My grandmother stated that she did not really consider it work. Maybe she was right. But was electrical cost estimating, which she did for many years, the best way to spend one's time on Earth either? Maybe we both did what we were good at.

There was a period in college when I got along well with my grandparents and visited them fairly often. They had by then moved to their A-frame house at 2526 Choccolocco Road. I usually came with my first wife, Mimi, whom they generally liked, I think. My grandmother only met Rika and my children once. That was also the last time I saw her alive. The children, very young, played in the creek by the A-frame where I had messed around as a kid. My grandmother seemed to greatly enjoy meeting them. I had sent her homemade calendars featuring their pictures for a couple of years, and she had these up on the fridge.

I did like the way Myrtice cooked, which was generally vegetable-based with very little meat, and that well-cooked. She canned a lot, and I liked the taste of that sort of boiled-to-hell-and-back vegetable far more than fresh vegetables, which I've never cottoned to. Her iced tea was always sweetened to within an inch of its life. I spoke the most with Emmett at that time, and that was when I found out what I know about their lives. Emmett often spoke of his time in World War II, and as he got older and the Alzheimer's kicked in, he became obsessed with discussing it for a time.

Emmett was in the U.S. Army in the Mediterranean theater. His Army serial number was 34977646, by the way. He went in already an electrician, and it was in the Army that he learned to wire buildings and structures on an industrial scale. He wired a Coca-Cola plant the Army built in Iran, for instance. The first Iraq war, and Operation Desert Storm, stirred up all those old memories in him one Christmas.

When he returned, he and Myrtice slowly turned Daniel Electric into a commercial and industrial contractor, and, from the 1950s on, eschewed wiring houses or domestic dwellings.

He had learned his original skills working for a man whose last name was Anthony. Somewhere there are photos of Emmett as a young man working for Anthony's company, I think. He was working for a place called Delta Electric prior to the war, according to a draft card. Perhaps this was Mr. Anthony's business.

Anyway, as Myrtice told me, this is where my father got his middle name. My grandmother liked the sound of Anthony and perhaps felt grateful to the Anthonys for getting her and Emmett off the farm, so she named my father Jerry Anthony. I became Jerry Anthony, II (later Jr.), and was eventually called Tony to differentiate me from my father. For quite a while, my Aunt Janice called me Anthony. My mother must have started off calling me that, but eventually it became Tony.

In the later 1940s, Emmett worked full time as an electrician at the iron foundry in Anniston, and worked part time for himself as he and my grandmother (who always did the office work and estimating) were building Daniel Electric. Eventually he employed ten or twenty workers, until the company went into decline in the 1960s as he and Myrtice seemed to lose interest in building it further. I think they took out a loan that taxed their ability to pay for several years during that time. I'm not sure what happened. Emmett was famously difficult to work for, and had a way of cursing terrifically on the job (a habit he may have picked up in the Army, I suppose).

It could also have been incipient Alzheimer's in my grandfather, even that far back. It is a strong trait in my paternal line. George. Emmett. Jerry. And I have the double allele for it waiting like a time bomb in my DNA.

One thing he was not good at was construction, but he continually built structures into his semi-retirement. They were always artful to look at but terribly put together. His floors creaked and his roofs leaked, and everything was drafty and cold. Yet who else in Anniston would have built an A-frame house to live in just because he liked the way it looked? He really liked that Frank Lloyd Wright influenced combination of industrial and homey. I'm quite sure my father and I got our artistic perception, at least partially, from Emmett. He actually was good at building rock walls from creek rock. Those were probably the only walls he ever built soundly. I liked the way his houses and outbuildings looked. They were original, and had a certain beauty.

He also shaped the Randolph County forty acres he'd inherited from his father, a valley with a little creek running through it, into a beautiful dell that seemed natural, but was the product of much thought and work. He had in him the makings of a Randolph County version of the great garden designer Capability Brown.

Emmett and Myrtice had also purchased eighty acres of cleared land nearby. As it grew back, they built a weekend cabin there where a spring and perhaps a homestead had been. Also on the eighty acres, as we called it, was an old copper mine test pit that my dog once almost fell into, thinking it was a pool of water. It was quite deep and scary when you came upon it gaping open like a maw in the woods. The cabin was eventually robbed and burned. I think that was a great loss for my grandmother, who, I believe, loved the place. That may have also marked the end of their social life beyond the family. I think they had friends from Anniston out there on weekends, but I don't remember them socializing when I was young.

By the mid-1950s, I think, they had moved into a house my grandfather built at 2911 Brighton Avenue, on the side of Blue Mountain, in Anniston.

Before that, they'd lived below the Daniel Electric shop at 2800 Noble Street, or nearby in a house at 5 W 28th Street (this later was a dwelling for Ben and Mollie Boalt, and maybe my grandmother's grandmother, Nora Creel Boalt Holsombeck, for a time).

My Aunt Patricia and her first husband, Roger Dulaney, lived in the little apartment under the Daniel Electric shop when I was very young. I remember playing with my cousin Cindy Dulaney and her half-sister (Roger's daughter) Karen there. This was while Roger and Patricia were getting their machine shop going, which eventually became Precision Tool and Machine. They later became government contractors for the military and beyond, producing screws and machine parts and such, and did quite well with it for a time.

The woods of Blue Mountain are what my father best remembers from his childhood. He and his friends played all over Blue Mountain and beyond. He has recorded audio of recollections of that time in his life, which I have, along with a great deal else from him. When he realized the Alzheimer's had hit him, and before he lost his memory, he sat down at his place in Centerville, Texas, and began recording what he considered his most interesting recollections. It's a treasure trove, and well worth a half-day of listening.

The Brighton Avenue house sat on a hillside overlooking a portion of north Anniston. I remember it as having rockers and rheostats for light switches—very unusual and advanced for the time—and big pane-less plate glass windows in the front. In other words, it had my grandfather's Frank Lloyd Wright influenced aesthetic. I liked it. Behind it was woods that went straight up the mountain. Cindy and I, and possibly my brother David, were playing back there when we were young and turned over some conduit my grandfather had stored there. That was when I was attacked by my first yellowjacket nest. I would get two more yellowjacket assaults (so far) in my life. One also occurred on the eighty acres, right where Emmett and Myrtice's old cabin used to be.

It is pretty clear that my father and I got our aesthetic sensibility from Emmett. He had a good eye and, while the houses he built were rickety and bow-legged after a few years, they were also wonders of design. The currents that fed Frank Lloyd Wright clearly flowed into my grandfather as well—those angular, utilitarian lines, the use of indigenous material from the countryside, building to fit the landscape and not modifying the land to fit the edifice. I have no idea if my grandfather ever heard of Wright, but there must have been something in the air in the early part of the twentieth century that both men partook of.

Obviously I have mixed feelings about Emmett O. Daniel. He was not a warm presence in my childhood. I hardly knew him. But he was not unkind in particular to me. After his death, I read some of his letters and even a journal-like entry he made for himself. He had a bit of a religious resurgence in the late 1980s, and wrote about how much he loved his grandchildren. But he was referring to Ricky and Sandy's children in the entry. I think he'd wholly forgotten about me and David as his grandchildren in particular by that point. When he was nearly eighty, he did go with Daddy, me, and my first wife, Mimi, on a trip to Big Bend National Park in Texas. He was already quite vague by that point, but it was a pleasant trip, I recall. He mostly looked at and admired nature. He got very cold when we were camping up in the mountains. I think this is the moment my dad realized his formerly tough-as-leather father had gotten quite frail.

I believe that Emmett's great strength was his aesthetic vision. He took his family on vacations to natural settings, especially the Smoky Mountains. He awakened my father's love of the landscape, and that was passed down to me. We went on an enormous, multi-vehicle, whole-family trip through the American West when I was perhaps seven years old, with my family, Patricia and Roger with Cindy and, I think Karen, and Ricky and Sandy, who were in their late teens and early twenties. Cindy and I had a great time, but Emmett argued constantly with Roger and my father, and he and Myrtice said hateful things to my mother on the trip, I later learned.

They looked down on Martha Montgomery in a class-based way, which was hilarious—the Montgomerys and Barrons as a whole are higher status clans than the Daniels. But I think, at base, they couldn't believe their shining first born son had to go and marry a coal miner's daughter. More the fools they.

Believe me, if it wasn't for my mother's resolve and ambition, my socially weak-willed father might never have done a damn thing with his life and would never have found the kind of fulfilment he eventually did by developing and making use of his drawing and artistic talent. The reason Jerry A. Daniel lacked fire and ambition was because Emmett and Myrtice had hectored it out of him when he was a child. It was always their way or the highway. And when he hit eighteen, it was the highway for him. I don't blame him.

Emmett was on the taller side, about five-eleven or even six feet, perhaps. He was always rail-thin, subsisting off my grandmother's canned vegetables and seemingly, white bread, pancakes and air. He was balding all the years I knew him, with close cropped gray hair on either side. He had light blue eyes like my father and myself. His eyesight was poor and he wore wireframed glasses, then plastic frame two-tone glasses later in life. He had a large mercury-arc lamppost fall on him in the 1970s when working at a Daniel Electric site (it was when Daniel Electric was wiring the then-new Anniston Winn Dixie grocery store parking lot), and it cut off a portion of one toe. This was, I think, the end of his full-time involvement with Daniel Electric. My uncle and father took over the job sites from there, although my grandmother stayed on in the office until the end.

After that, he devoted more and more time to his hobby farm in Randolph County, where he kept a herd of cows that he never sold, and planted no crop other than an occasional garden.

Grandaddy in general did not like to kill animals. He didn't fish. He did not hunt. I believe this was a philosophical decision on his part, since I think his father and his other relatives did hunt. He didn't teach my father to hunt, and so I never got any instruction in it either. I think it was also a bit of a class distinction. He had moved to town and was a city man, not a farmer, in his own eyes. Yet he continued to tinker in the country whenever he got a chance.

For a time, he thought he was going to develop a campground. He bought some land near an I-20 exit east of Anniston and was developing it, building some buildings, even, and laying out spaces. I have no idea what happened, but it didn't come to fruition, and he eventually sold off the land. I think even in the 70s, his incipient Alzheimer's was affecting him and he couldn't work toward a long term plan anymore.

This is one of the reasons Daniel Electric declined—but also it was fatally wounded by the fact that, after ten years back working with his parents, my father left to work at Hunt Oil as a cartographer in 1982. He continued at Hunt for twenty-four years after that until he retired. My father and, to some extent my uncle, Ricky, had become the face of the company, interacting with architects and clients, and keeping the workers, who were not paid a great deal, generally happy. As I said, my grandfather developed a reputation as an irascible cuss to work with and there were architects, electrical engineers, and contractors in Anniston who refused to deal with him, but liked my dad (and no doubt respected my grandmother's accurate bids). My uncle Ricky continued on a while after, but eventually left to go into land surveying, and the company dissolved.

During his 70s, Emmett was working on his Randolph County place, driving a tractor, when he hit a stump and the tractor turned over on him, shattering his collar bone, among other injuries. He was unable to stand up, but had to crawl and drag his way back to the house, where for several hours he attempted to call my grandmother. She was out on errands. He was in and out of consciousness, but finally reached her and was taken to the hospital. It took him months, but he did recover. Like my father, his health, other than his brain, was remarkable throughout his life. His collar bone remained dislocated however, and caused him to have trouble speaking without a slightly phlegmy sound and throat clearing thereafter.

Several years before that, in the 1980s, I think, he was bitten by a black widow spider, didn't realize it, and eventually had to go into the hospital for at least a couple of weeks, his life touch and go. This was another near-death from which he bounced back remarkably. Emmett was a tough man.

My grandparents retired to the A-frame on Choccolocco Road which Emmett had built himself (with the exception of hanging the drywall, which he hated doing), and to the two or three acres—containing a nice pond they put in—that it sat upon. At one time they attempted to expand the pond, but the water table wouldn't allow it. I believe they'd had the creek that ran through the property dug out into a ditch-like run to expose more rocks and make some little rapids (which my grandparents liked). This lowered the water table, however, and doomed the lake expansion. They spent years trying to make that lake work after that, but a portion usually sat dry and rather ugly. But what I best remember is the original small pond there, and the little green boat we could take out into the water. My grandfather kept fish in the lake, which he fed and never attempted to catch. He was not a fisherman, and I don't think my grandmother liked to cook fish, anyway.

We kept a grown pony and a colt pony, Winnie and Bitsy, in the back pasture of the A-frame for a couple of years until my grandmother badgered my mother into getting rid of them. They themselves kept a roan Shetland pony there for many years named Lucky. He was a bastard and would charge and bite you. I hated him. The very back of that pasture became our dog graveyard for a time, and it holds my first dog, Frisky, the Pomeranian that was my mother's favorite, Fluffy, the scrappy, smelly halfbreed Ping, and several others brought back from Texas later and reverentially laid to rest there. My father welded a couple of metal crosses for them that were beautiful examples of outsider art (or whatever they are calling non-establishment art these days).

My grandfather was basically dying of Alzheimer's for a good ten years, from about 1998 onward, and my grandmother cared for him. I didn't see him during this time. He was debilitated and staying in the A-frame bedroom almost exclusively. He is buried in the Smyrna Church graveyard near Newell in Randolph County.

My overall impression of Emmett Daniel is that he was a driven, gifted man with a sharp mind and a well-honed sense of the beautiful, as well as a soft side he seldom showed. He was physically resilient, which probably served him well in World War II, and certainly did later. I think he was determined from a young age to get off the farm and do something interesting with his life, and he achieved this. He had an intense middle period of his life where he and my grandmother were socially engaged in town and in professional organizations, followed by a mellow, quirky last three decades spent alone with his thoughts and projects. He and my grandmother returned to their religious roots toward the end of their lives, and started going back to church, which they hadn't ever attended while I was growing up. My love for him is mostly admiration rather than warm regard, but I greatly appreciate his strong points, and I thank him for passing some of them on.

My research has turned up more supposed relatives beyond Isaac Beck Daniel and Elizabeth Lovvorn, but I'll have to wait for DNA evidence to confirm anything. Back to him, I'm fairly sure of the line. I don't know much about Susan Dorrough, Isaac Elijah's wife, or her family, or about Elizabeth Williams, Hart Daniel's wife.

I don't know a great deal more about the Daniel side of the family. Basically they were Northwest Alabama residents for two hundred years. Farmers until my grandfather adapted to the twentieth century by becoming an electrician. You have to have seen how country my ancestors were, which I did, to fully grasp the profound change in lifestyle Emmett and Myrtice underwent in the mid-twentieth century. I think it didn't so much happen to them as they chose it, too. But until then, it was a country life for my Daniel ancestors. Most worked the American soil as far back as I can presently trace. Not one was a nineteenth century immigrant. They seem to have been in America for the last 250 years, and maybe more.

The Boalts

My paternal grandmother's maiden name was Myrtice Magdalene Boalt. She went by "Myrtice," spoken MUHRtis, almost as one syllable. "Boalt" sounds like "Bolt," with the "a" sitting silent among the other letters, never voiced, but always present as a mark of distinction. I never heard my grandmother once say her middle name, so I don't know how she pronounced that.

Benjamin Franklin Boalt (1903-1977)

I knew my grandmother's father and her step-mother, Molly. My mother often told me that my grandmother's actual mother, Ruth Whitmore Boalt (1905-1963), had been a sweet woman—and sweet in more ways than one, for she developed diabetes and, I heard elsewhere, could not stop herself eating sweets, even when she knew it was likely killing her.

Her husband, Benjamin Franklin Boalt (1903-1977), was a farmer—a hog farmer for some years. I remember going out to his house and farm and returning home unable to get the smell of stinking pigs out of my nostrils. For those who say that pigs are falsely maligned and are actually very clean animals, I can only reply that they never visited Pa Boalt's place.

Ben Boalt didn't seem to own his land. He rented and moved around a lot. He ended up in a small clapboard house near Morris Crossroads in Randolph County. As he got older and his emphysema grew worse, he kept the place warmer and warmer during the cool months, constantly feeding his small woodstove. He, and his second wife

Molly Prince Boalt, who was very kind, would sit rocking and violently coughing together during our visits. Bursting outside into the cool air after we were done was a kind of physical epiphany for my body. Pa Boalt finally died of emphysema. He looked like a wax dummy at his funeral. I noticed that he had no nose hairs—and he had always had plenty of them in life. Perhaps the undertaker trimmed them.

My cousin Cindy and her step-sister Karen were there at the funeral, and my brother David and I played with them in the dust of the churchyard. I only realized that Pa Boalt was truly gone when we went to visit Molly and the house was heated to a normal temperature.

Nora Creel Boalt Holsombeck (1868-1954)

I don't know a lot about the Boalts. I'm not sure when the "a" got added. Most Boalts in the family tree went by "Bolt." With or without the "a," I think Ben Boalt's father and his mother came to Alabama from Georgia. According to my grandmother, Pa Boalt didn't know much about his father's side of his heritage. His dad, James Riley Boalt (1857-1920), died when he was around eighteen. His mother, Nora Creel Boalt Holsombeck, remarried and lived many more years, but, according to my father, told my grandmother that she had never learned much about her husband's family. Her father was named Benjamin, and they may have named Pa Boalt after him.

When Nora was widowed again, she came to live in the little house next to the Daniel Electric shop, 5 W 28th Street. Or perhaps she lived below the shop in the small apartment. My father remembered her as appearing very old and frail to him, "Granny Holsombeck was as old as the hills," he said to me. She died when he was around fourteen. She was eighty-six by then.

Myrtice Magdalene Boalt Daniel (1921-2012)

Emmett and Myrtice Daniel married in the 1930s. Just before the Second World War, they had my father, Jerry Anthony. My grandfather went into the Army and traveled to the Mediterranean theatre. He was in North Africa, Iran, and Iraq. I'm not sure what Myrtice was doing during that time other than raising my father. I heard details once of how they traveled to Miami and met my grandfather there. And I believe they travelled to New York City during the war, as well. I also know Myrtice drove to Fort Leonard Wood in Missouri to visit Emmett. She travelled there using gas ration coupons she'd earned from driving neighbors in Newell around on errands using her relatively new car.

After the war, Emmett and Myrtice started (or perhaps continued) Daniel Electric in Anniston, which was a town of about thirty thousand at the time, in Calhoun County, Alabama, two counties northwest of Randolph County, Alabama, with a slice of Cleburne County between them. Calhoun and Cleburne Counties were once part of a single county called Benton County, by the way—named after Thomas Hart Benton, a U.S. senator from Missouri, who flipped from pro- to anti-slavery during the 1850s. The inhabitants changed the name in 1858. My father created a map of the old Benton County, and we sold it at craft fairs along with his great Alabama 1823 map. More on that later.

Myrtice was as much the driving force in Daniel Electric as Emmett was. She did the estimating and cost accounting. She created the bids for commercial work, and was very honest about it—and yet very good at coming in low and winning the projects she was after. Architects and general contractors knew they could trust Daniel Electric bids, something one couldn't say about all contractors. During the 1950s and 1960s, my grandmother was involved with the Women in Construction organization, and I think she once held a regional office in WIC.

Emmett and Myrtice had four more children, but one was stillborn. This was Emmett O. Daniel, Jr., in 1943. The baby is buried at Smyrna churchyard, and I don't know anything else about him. After that were Patricia, Sandy, and Ricky. Patricia was born in 1947, after the war was over and Emmett and Myrtice permanently reunited. She married Roger Dulaney (1945-2008) and they had my favorite cousin, Cynthia Lynette Dulaney, in 1964. Cindy is now a professor of psychology at Xavier University in Cincinnati with two children.

Sandra Joyce Daniel (born 1950) took a while to settle down. She went to Utah for several summers and worked a staff job at Bryce

Canyon National Park. We visited her there on one of our Western vacations. Sandy eventually married Jeff Cooke and has two daughters. She later developed the terrible Early Onset Alzheimer's and poor Jeff has been living with that for many years now, as, of course, has Sandy.

Ricky Carl Daniel (born 1951), who now goes by a manly "Rick," married Jan Parker, and had a daughter and son, Lacey and Adam, before he and Jan divorced. He married Diane Acker some years later, and became the stepfather to Diane's kids.

My grandparents did fairly well with Daniel Electric during the earlier years. They lived in the house on Blue Mountain, and eventually moved to the A-frame a bit out from Anniston on Choccolocco Road near the Golden Springs subdivision where I spent my teen years. My grandfather built the A-frame himself (except, as I've mentioned, for hanging the sheetrock plasterboard—he tried and the sheetrock kept breaking. Cursing and swearing up a storm, as was his wont, he called up a professional service and had it done for him.). My father spent his youngest years in Anniston on the alleged wrong end of Noble Street (the northern end), the main street through downtown (although Quintard Avenue later became the real main drag of Anniston). I think the move to Brighton Avenue was also, in a sense, a move up in social status in that very stratified town.

My father was always interested in the intersection of technology and landscape. Maybe wandering the back side of Blue Mountain, which overlooked the Army's enormous Fort McClellan, awakened this in him. He described the view there as a mixed vista of hardwood and pine woodland strewn with Army vehicles blasted to interesting scrap in the training area there. And he, no doubt, got this fascination from his parents, as well. He joined the Civil Air Patrol and, at a CAP teen mixer at Maxwell Air Force Base in Montgomery, he met my mother, Martha Ann Montgomery.

After high school, Jerry went to college at Auburn for a semester. Emmett and Myrtice sent him contingent upon his studying electrical engineering. Jerry had other plans, and he asked his parents if he could undertake a different course of study. They refused, and furthermore told him that if he changed his major, they would not help with his tuition or board.

I believe this was a major psychological breaking point between my father and his demanding parents, although he would always retain the connection, later working for, and with, them for a decade while I was a teen. But he did not want to be an electrical engineer, and he did not want to go to Auburn to do it. He was done trying to live up to Emmett and Myrtice's expectations.

Jerry had been dating Martha during his year at Auburn and, instead of truckling under to Emmett and Myrtice, he eloped with Martha that summer. They had a shotgun, late-night wedding across the Georgia line in Trenton. He quit Auburn. Then Jerry and Martha took off for Tampa, Florida, where they lived for about a year and a half, I believe. My mother got a job at the Indian River Fruit Exchange, and my father worked as a draftsman. They eventually decided to return to Alabama and go to college.

They moved to Tuscaloosa, where both of them entered the University of Alabama—and paid their own way. Jerry got a part-time job at the state Geological Survey. This led him to a job at the U.S. Geological Survey, and to a major in geology, with a minor in math. He was to become a professional cartographer. Martha would take another twenty years to finish up her college degree, matriculating in 1987 at Jacksonville State University, north of Anniston.

Emmett and Myrtice functioned as a unit. This could be a product of years of marriage, but I have a feeling they were always soulmates—both of them were work-oriented, choleric, and sometimes narrowly judgmental of others to an astonishing degree. They built Daniel Electric together, my grandmother doing the estimating, bidding, and bookkeeping, my grandfather doing the on-site work. They also drove it into the ground together. They were Baptists, but their true religion was a kind of literal fundamentalist worship of Work. This Work was a sweating god, a god of unremitting toil. A god with a vicious streak when it came to those who were not of the faith.

At times, I have tried to empathize with this less admirable side of Emmett and Myrtice because it so greatly affected my father. I believe they felt surrounded by those they conceived of as lazy and misguided. They were constantly driven to activity, even if it was merely picking up rocks in a wheelbarrow and moving them from one side of their land to the other. It was a strange blend of self-abnegation and hubris that eventually sent my father Jerry in a very different direction.

Myrtice was striking, pretty in an intense way when she was young, with big, expressive eyes. You see it in her photos. She had very dark hair and had, I think I recall, brown eyes. She was a small woman, always thin and in good shape from working outside. For most of her life, she smoked like a chimney, as did Emmett, but they did quit. I think she had a bout of breast cancer that she overcame.

In most ways, Myrtice Daniel was a decent and kind woman. I judged her pretty harshly when I was younger because my mother simply couldn't stand her. It was like an allergic reaction. My mother would begin shaking with both anxiety and resentment whenever she had to have much to do with Myrtice, whom she always called "Mrs. Daniel." My mother never had this attitude toward anyone else in her life, and is otherwise a wellspring of sympathy. Something very bad must have happened between the two at some point to produce in my mother this continuing reaction. Knowing them both, I'm quite sure my grandmother was entirely to blame. I don't know if my mother has ever wittingly hurt another in her life, and I know my grandmother made some bitter comments to me and my brother over the years.

David and I had started off calling her "Memaw," as we did Louise Montgomery, my maternal grandmother. Myrtice didn't like this, and eventually instructed me and David to call her "Grandmother" and not "Me-maw." It took me some time to make the switch.

I should add a strong caveat here. My cousin, Cindy Dulaney, who is the closest thing I have to a sister, has what I think is a different perception of Emmett—and especially Myrtice. I can't speak for Cindy, but I know she had a strong maternal connection to Myrtice—I witnessed it in action—and, for her, Myrtice was an archetypical grandmotherly presence. There was a soft side of Myrtice that I think was reserved for Cindy, in particular.

I'm afraid I will always see my grandmother through the lens of my parents. Yet I did grow up and away from the narrowed perception of childhood. In later years, my attitude toward my grandmother softened. She was an only child, and always carried that single child lonesomeness and innate self-dependence with her, it seemed to me. It must've been a very tough childhood clawing her way from relative poverty in Randolph County—I mean, Pa Boalt seemed to own nothing but his clothes—and I'm sure she wanted to make sure her own family never had to experience anything like that themselves. She was tough and resourceful, and I'm proud to have her as my grandmother.

Part 2
The
Montgomery Branch

Coker and Louise Montgomery

I have a very different impression of my maternal grandparents. They were loving, pushy, talkative people. My grandfather was clever and a bit of a trickster. He is my favorite relative, and I named my daughter after him. Most of all, he was a gifted storyteller. My grandmother was equally smart, a bit self-serving at times, but also extremely giving and protective of her small brood. She was a hairdresser for much of her life, creating those amazing teased beehive doos from the 1950s and 1960s for her customers. For quite a while, she and my Aunt Janice ran a beauty shop together, mostly in the Tarrant City neighborhood of Birmingham, Alabama. I remember playing in it with David as a child. I think I wreaked havoc trying to rearrange everything. I took a proprietary interest in the place. My grandmother and aunt basically let me run rampant, until my mother finally stopped me. Needless to say, this could not have happened around my Daniel grandparents.

Coker

‹•➤═◑⊂═•›

James Coker Montgomery (1914-1990)

What I know about James Coker Montgomery is a good deal shrouded by his legend within my own mind. He was not named Coker when he was born, but initially named George on his birth certificate. That didn't last long. His parents at first called him James Kerby Montgomery, or "Curvey," which I saw him sign once when I was little, maybe just to amuse me. But eventually everyone called him Coker, except the guys at work, who called him Monk. In 1973, he had the state of Alabama officially correct his birth name to James Coker. The reason I believe he acquired this name, a story which he verified to some extent, was that when his mother died he was very young. He was sent to live with relatives in the town of Coker, Alabama. When he returned home for good some years later, everyone called him Coker, because he was, for them, the kid from Coker. There is, however, a Coker last name in the family tree of his mother, Elizabeth Skelton. Her grandmother's name was Huldah Coker. So Lizzie Skelton Montgomery would have been aware of that name. Coker said he didn't like the name "Kerby" or "Curvey." One might conjecture that it was what his mother called him, and when he heard it, he missed her. But this I do not know.

In any case, James C. Montgomery was Coker for the rest of his life.

After 1925 or so, he grew up in a little town that I'm not even sure was a real incorporated entity, in Tuscaloosa County. It was called Brownville. It was a mill village. In fact, it was a clump of houses built around a large creosote pole production plant. The houses were

31

arranged in a square around the processing yard and plant. It was as pungent as it sounds. I visited when it was still in operation, and creosote poles, dripping in the sun, were stacked in neat piles in an enormous yard, awaiting delivery everywhere.

Brownville was only founded in the mid 1920s, however. Coker didn't spend his youngest years there. For many years, his father, Taylor Montgomery, was a farmer. The story that Coker told me is this: in the late 1910s or early 1920s, Taylor Montgomery took out a loan from a bank in order to buy a team of mules. As collateral against that purchase he put up his land, thinking he would surely be able to pay the money back. However, the mules took sick and died, and he was unable to meet the terms of the loan. The bank foreclosed on his property and took it away. I believe my grandfather told me this occurred in the early twenties. For some reason, 1922 sticks in my mind. So this may have occurred just after he married Fannie Skelton, his second wife.

So Taylor lost my great-grandmother, his first wife, to the Spanish Flu, in 1919, when he was forty-two and she was thirty-eight. Then he lost his oldest son, Sellie, four years later to peritonitis. He might have felt like a cursed man for a time. Imagine, poor Taylor thinking he'd made a new start after the death of his wife, only to forfeit his land. And then, perhaps a year later, his oldest son dies in the hospital. Whatever their order, calamities hit Taylor Montgomery like a deluge for a few years there.

In the 1920 census, Taylor is a widower living on a farm. Then in the 1930 census, Taylor is living in Brownville. I think he must have had to seek employment there after losing the farm. Interestingly, the 1930 census lists Taylor's occupation as "blacksmith," and his place of employment as "shop."

He cast about for something to do, and got a job working for the Brown company, but not at the creosote mill. In fact, I don't believe Taylor Montgomery ever worked at that mill. The reason that Brownville was called Brownville was because it was owned by the Brown Lumber Company, which belonged to a family named Brown. It had nothing to do with the color of the creosote poles, which was also brown. And all the houses in town were brown, of course, being made from creosote wood, except for the central all-purpose church, which was clapboard white.

Anyway, Taylor took the job of being a woodcutter, according to Coker Montgomery. He went out into the forests nearby (what would be the Sipsey Wilderness) and cut and hauled posts that would be used to make fences around the Brown family orchards. The family maintained a tract of them at the company town, according to my grandfather. In my mind, Taylor was the local factotum, the keeper of the boundaries, the builder and maintainer of fences. Probably he was an excellent repair man, too, if my own grandfather's incredible ability as an auto mechanic is any indication.

In any case, it was in his early teenage years that Coker Montgomery moved to Brownville. Taylor, Fannie and the boys, then Maria, when she came along, lived in house 51 on the Brownville loop of creosote houses. There were three sections of housing. One was the supervisors and managers, who had indoor plumbing after a time. The second was the white families, such as the Montgomerys. The other was a group of shotgun houses a little separated, which housed the black families. Both white and black families had outhouses. All the houses were heated with coal or wood. But everyone who lived in them had a job through the Great Depression, which was the great worth of Brownville.

As with the housing, in Brownville, there was a two-tiered system in the creosote mill. The black people generally worked in the dipping area, the most dangerous and smelly part of the operation. The white people worked in the yard doing the other tasks. It was all very hard work, whatever it was. I'm sure no one got paid much and they were probably charged against whatever they bought at the company store, etc., although I never heard from my grandfather that anyone felt exploited. I think they were glad to have the work, especially during the Depression. My grandfather was determined never to be employed in that factory long term, however.

Coker hunted a great deal as a young man. In the mill, he had some friends who were black and worked there. When he went out hunting, he would sometimes bring them food that he had shot—particularly squirrels and rabbits. One time as a teenager he had brought some rabbits to someone in the dipping vat area.

"I got to playing around above the vat and fell partly in," he told me. He dropped into the scalding creosote. They had to carry him home and he was several weeks recuperating.

It is an interesting fact that mosquitoes never seemed to bother my grandfather during the time I knew him. I've often wondered if this could be attributed to the fact that he took that creosote dip when he was a teenager. Maybe not.

Coker got a job as a woodcutter and mule driver when he became old enough to work, which was around the age of thirteen or fourteen, I believe. He never went beyond sixth grade in school. He read adequately and was always working through the *Birmingham News* when I knew him. He did not read many books that I know of. My other grandfather, Emmett was a reader of books. He particularly liked Westerns, and adored the Foxfire series of nonfiction collections on Appalachian life and crafts.

Anyway, Coker always told me that wood cutting in the Sipsey Swamp was the hardest work he'd ever done. They hauled it with horses or mules, and then put it on a small train. These operated on spur lines that ran out into the wilderness.

As some point, I know that he was working at Brownville or for the Browns, because he got fired from there.

This is another iconic story of Coker Montgomery that I kind of remember but have perhaps embellished in my mind. I originally got the gist of it from Coker himself. He and a friend decided they were going to Tuscaloosa one night, and they absconded with one of the single-car motor driven train wagons that the Brownville company possessed. They took it into Tuscaloosa and found someplace to drink and carouse for a few hours. Then they headed back. But it ran out of gas before it got all the way to Brownville—somewhere far up the tracks. Coker and his friend had to walk home several miles. Of course they had to leave the train car in place for someone to get. When he straggled in that morning, he was met by the Brownville foreman, a man named Langston. As my grandfather put it, "Old Man Langston told me he hated to do it, but he was going to have to fire me for that. I felt pretty bad, but it turned out to be the best thing that ever happened to me. It got me out of Brownville for good."

Langston was the father of a long-time television news anchor in Birmingham, Alabama, by the way. My grandfather pointed that out to me once.

Another story my grandfather told me was of going frog gigging in the Sipsey Swamp. He was out with yet another friend one night. They were gigging by lantern light when they passed under a low hanging branch. Suddenly, a snake plopped from the branch into the boat. Coker was afraid it was a water moccasin.

He and his friend began to scramble, and they overturned the boat. Quickly, they were both in the water splashing around, each knowing that snake was somewhere nearby. My grandfather said it was some of the scaredest he'd ever been. They did get back un-snakebit. But also without a light.

Coker eventually moved to Brookside, Alabama. He did not want to go into the coal mines there, and I believe that he was actually on a crew cutting wood in the forest nearby for a time. He put his profession down on his marriage license as "mule driver."

At the Brookside mines area, he met a man who evidently recognized Coker's native intelligence. The fellow told him he would get Coker a job in the mine as an electrician and would ensure that he never had to mine coal directly. My grandfather took the man at his word and went into the coal mines there at Brookside.

And that is what happened. Coker became an electrician in the coal mines. He was trained to do the wiring that was required down there. I'm sure he picked it up very quickly. He was extremely adept at mechanical and electrical matters.

It was a big distinction in his mind that he didn't mine coal himself, but was responsible for the machinery. I believe this was a status and pay distinction in the mines, as well. This also allowed him to later get a job in the steel mills when he got tired of going down in the hole. He spent most of his life as an electrician in Birmingham iron and steel mills, for U.S. Steel, and for U.S. Pipe at Sloss Furnace in Birmingham.

My impressions of Birmingham are highly complex. I spent many years there. First, I went to visit my grandparents while I was growing up in Tuscaloosa and Anniston. Then I went to college there. It is a post-Civil War city. There was no Birmingham during the Civil War. It was built on iron and steel. There was coal in the hills nearby, and there was iron ore in the great mountain that stands over the valley where the city would be built. That is Red Mountain. In the valley below Red Mountain, a large iron industry bloomed. It took off by the end of the 1800s, and there was a point when Birmingham rivaled its northern analogues, such as Pittsburgh. The issue with Birmingham, and the problem with the political class of Birmingham, was the fact that most of the iron industry there was controlled by northern interests. The men who ran the plants and foundries in Birmingham were sent down from Pittsburgh and elsewhere. They did not sink deep roots into the area, but were working for promotions and a return north. For decades, there was no well-to-do upper class deeply invested in the town.

There are plenty of old, monied families in Birmingham now, but nothing like the aristocracy of Georgia, or even that of South Alabama. In the end, I believe that this probably doomed the city to second-class status next to Atlanta. That and the fact that Atlanta gambled big on expanding its airport at just the right time to become a worldwide hub of commerce.

In the early 1960s, there was civil rights unrest. Protests. Bombings. Death. Firehoses. Police dogs threatening children. This permanently tainted the image of the city. But that era is practically ancient history now. All of the city's mayors have been black since the late 1970s. Growing up in and around Birmingham, I scarcely gave the civil rights history a thought because it had nothing to do with me. It was done. I was born after all that. The city had moved on. To pretend otherwise was to nurse a false romanticism, to simplify and degrade.

Of course, the city was a very different place under segregation, and that's when many of my ancestors who lived in the area were there. But seeing how my grandparents interacted with everyone around them, I think life was far more interesting than some racial morality play.

When I went to college, it was at the tail-end of the steel mill era. The last of them was shutting down, but there were still some in operation. Sloss Furnace operated. U.S. Pipe existed, in its Jim Walter Industries incarnation. But in the late 60s and early 70s, when we came in from the Tuscaloosa side of Birmingham through Fairfield, there were days when the air was so thick with smoke from the mills that it was like a pea soup fog. You could not see through it. And you had to come in on city streets. For many years, the interstate from Tuscaloosa into Birmingham was incomplete because the city never fully supported George Wallace in elections, and he delayed funding.

Fairfield and Ensley stank. They stank and you could roll your windows down, roll your windows up, nothing could keep out the smell. It permeated the car. It got into your throat and eyes.

By the time I went to college at Birmingham-Southern, the thick smog of Fairfield was dissipated. But, if you had a white car, you would still get the mill smoke build-up on it within a day or two. You couldn't wash your car enough to keep that residue off. You just learned to live with it. Then, over the course of my college years there, from 1982 to 1986, the soot disappeared as the final mills closed down.

But Birmingham didn't die. It didn't die as everyone predicted it would. Instead, the biomedical industry surrounding the University of Alabama at Birmingham bloomed. Other tech and financial companies moved into business parks in the periphery. Today Birmingham is a green and fairly pretty city. I'm amazed at the transformation.

Standing over the city atop Red Mountain is the great statue of the forge god himself, Vulcan, his gigantic bare buttocks mooning Homewood. He holds a raised electric torch that shines at night. During my childhood, the torch was used to indicate whether anyone had been killed in a traffic related death in the past twenty-four hours. The torch burned green when nobody died. It turned red when they had. Eventually the city halted this macabre display. I miss it. I always thought it was the only real reason to live in Birmingham to start with.

It was when he was in Brookside that Coker came across my grandmother. Louise Cooley was rather young, I think around sixteen, at the time. He was nine years older than she was. I can imagine how cute my grandmother must've been at that age. She was always extremely engaged with keeping up her appearance, and I think she must've been quite a looker in her teen years.

The problem, or at least the situation, with my grandmother was that if you married Louise Cooley, you had to take her mother, Electa. My Mama Cooley, as I called her, my great-grandmother Electa Barron Cooley, had been a widow since 1924. She had no place else to stay except with her daughter, whom she'd raised as an only child after her other boy (or boys, I'm not sure exactly what happened there) died just about the same year as her husband did. It was a horrific tragedy, and my great-grandmother never talked about it with me, or really, anyone.

My grandfather, to his credit, agreed to take Electa Cooley in along with Louise when he married her. Or, to put it precisely, *they* agreed to take *Coker* in. He moved into their house. And, for the rest of their lives, those three lived together. My grandfather died first, then Electa Cooley, and finally my grandmother, Louise Montgomery Poe, who died with me holding her hand and listening to her last breath.

So Coker and Louise Montgomery began their life together.

Coker took up with Mama Cooley's sister's husband, James Gibb, and became drinking buddies with him. Uncle Jimmy and Coker used to go on legendary benders. Uncle Jimmy was known to be a very mean drunk. He was quite abusive toward my Aunts Betty and Barbara, I heard. But by the time I knew him, and as long as I knew my grandfather, both men had given up drinking entirely. Uncle Jimmy was one of the nicest fellows you would ever want to meet. Aunt Mae was incredibly sweet. She was the baby of the Barron girls. I spent several hours with them when I was in college, as they lived nearby, and I attended Uncle Jimmy's funeral. It was hard for me to reconcile the man I knew with what I'd heard from my mother, and from Coker himself, about his drinking days. Those stories were one of the reasons I decided never to risk becoming a heavy drinker myself.

My grandfather did smoke, and he smoked incessantly. He was a chain smoker of Pall Malls when I was younger, and then Marlboro Reds when I was older, and finally Marlboro Lights at some point. All of my memories of being with him are shot through with the odor of cigarette smoke. That is one of the reasons that I do not mind the odor, and also one of the reasons I think that the risk of secondary smoke is overblown. If anybody was going to get cancer from secondary smoke, it would be me, because I hung around my grandfather's secondhand smoke for years.

Coker was a dark complexioned man, with coal-black hair. He had blue eyes, however. Even into his older age, he dyed his hair with Grecian Formula to keep it black. It was only when he got sick and was unable to do this that the gray was revealed. It stayed thick, and he never balded in any manner. I think he was pretty proud of that thatch of hair he had. It was also wavy, as mine became after I hit puberty. I think I probably have him to blame for that.

Coker tanned very easily, and grew very dark when he did. This is something that my mother and myself have inherited. He looked in many ways like Humphrey Bogart in some lights. He was five-foot-ten-inches. His skin was stippled with mole-like freckles, widely spread. My aunt Janice, who was a redhead, was extremely freckled as well. No one is quite sure where Janice's complexion came from, but there is no doubt she is Coker and Louise's child. Her redheaded looks bothered Janice for her entire life. She sometimes referred to herself as the "redheaded stepchild," in fact. It is interesting how differently complexioned my mother and her sister were.

For most of Coker's working life he wore the uniform of U.S. Steel, U.S. Pipe, and the coal mines—that is, the mono-colored Dickies pants and trousers. This was either a khaki-colored pair of pants and top, or a dark gray-blue shirt and pants. The shirt was collared and had breast pockets where Coker put his cigarettes. He always carried a pair of pliers and a flatblade screwdriver in one back pocket. This mono-colored outfit was what he wore almost every day except on Sunday. Sometimes he also had coveralls that were of that charcoal blue color, as well. He liked to wear the charcoal blue more than khakis; I think he believed it looked better on him. But he wore khakis plenty, too. It was a uniform that set him off as a dignified workingman, and he was proud of dressing that way. He always wore black shoes, as I recall, laced. He was never a boot man.

He sometimes wore a brown flannel shirt and work pants—I never saw him in a pair of blue jeans—when off duty. But even after he retired, he was often in his former work clothes.

Coker wore a watch on an expandable steel band. Emmett's watch was attached to a dark leather band, by the way. I always felt this said something about both their characters. Coker wore a wedding ring.

One thing Coker had was dentures—that is, a complete set of false teeth. Early on, he'd had all of his teeth pulled and wore those things for most of his life. So did my great-grandmother, Electa Cooley. I believe that Coker regretted not having at least some of his teeth. His dentures sometimes pained him, and often at home he would not put them in.

As I've mentioned, Coker was very good at working on cars. It was his hobby and his passion when he wasn't at the furnace. The other thing that he and Louise liked to do very much was go on vacation in Florida. I don't know when they found Clearwater, Florida, but they loved to go down there and stay in a hotel for a couple weeks every year. I think the only vacation they ever took was going to Florida. I went down there twice with them at very different ages. Coker enjoyed going places where he knew the proprietor. He stayed in the exact same hotel, and was friendly with the motel owner when he went to Clearwater. He enjoyed being recognized as a regular.

He was, in general, a very social man. He could fit in easily, talk with any crowd. He was extremely curious and asked people questions. Above all, he could tell a story. He knew how to do a set-up, how to structure his tale so that it had a beginning, middle, end, and a climax. He sometimes threw in a twist at the end. He was a consummate storyteller, and I learned a great deal just sitting and listening to him. Maybe all I ever needed to know.

One thing he didn't like to talk about much was his mother. He really didn't remember her well, but he felt resentful of her for leaving him by dying—even though he knew that he should not feel this way. I think when he was young he was really mad at her for not being there, and sometimes that feeling would come back to him as an adult in an overwhelming manner. I think he also really missed her throughout his life. I also believe that growing up basically orphaned for many years during his childhood is what led him to drinking later.

When Lizzie Skelton died, Coker was five years old. She died in 1919 of the Spanish Flu. The story is that she was tending some neighbors who had come down with it, and she caught the disease herself and was dead soon after, maybe a couple of days. Coker was born in 1914. He was very young when she died, yet old enough to remember her.

She's very lovely, and in the surviving picture I've seen, she bears a resemblance to my mother, and to Cokie, my daughter, I think. So Lizzie Skelton was gone in 1919, and Coker had to grow up with just his father, Taylor—and eventually with his new stepmother, whom he came to love, Frances Skelton (1885-1971). They married in April of 1922. Lizzie had died in early February, three years earlier.

Frances—Fannie, as I believe she was called—was perhaps a cousin of Lizzie, but it is a distant relationship. They were not related directly in any way that I heard of, and I did ask. Taylor and Frances went on to have two more children, a half-brother and half-sister to Coker and his brother Revis. These children were Maria Montgomery (1923-2017) and Baines Taylor Montgomery (1925-2008). Maria, of course, became one of my favorite aunts. I spent many hours with her and her husband Gene when I lived in Los Angeles and went to film school there. Gene got me a job while I was out there managing a ministorage warehouse, which helped me pay for my film school tuition and gave me a place to live.

Coker had another brother, and Lizzie and Taylor had another son, their oldest. His name was Sellie Montgomery (1905-1923). Sellie died in 1923. He was evidently working at the time as an attendant at Bryce Hospital, which was the State of Alabama's insane asylum for many decades.

The way that I understand it was that he had something like an appendectomy or some other sort of gastrointestinal operation. He woke up from it in the hospital where he'd had the procedure, and felt extremely thirsty. Nearby was a pitcher of water, and he drank all of it. Perhaps his intestine was perforated at the time, or healing and stitched up. All I know for sure is that, according to his obituary, he died of peritonitis. The rest is the story I heard from my mother and others.

Sellie was eighteen years old when he died, so Coker knew him well. His other brother, Revis, grew up to become a coal miner. Revis eventually moved to Kentucky, where he worked in the mines for many years, married, and had a large family that still lives there. We went through once, and I met him before he died. He bore a strong resemblance to Grandaddy, of course, but his face was longer, more drawn out.

Coker was an amazing gardener. He could make just about anything grow, and he liked to have a garden near his house. At one point, my mother tells me, he came out of the mines and decided he was going to be a farmer. He bought some terrible, nonproductive land near Brookside with a polluted creek running through it. My mother remembers it.

Coker tried to farm for a year or so. But he was also drinking at the time, and it was not a good idea in the end. Because I believe the creek came from a tailings pit, his crops didn't grow. It was chemically tainted water.

A sad tale comes from that time. My mother had a dog while she was out there, and my grandfather told me a terrible story about that. It was a little fitch, as he called it. He never liked it because he always thought it looked at him in an insolent, arrogant manner. He said he didn't know why he thought the dog was gazing at him like that, but he didn't like it.

So one day he was sitting on his porch drinking, in fact quite drunk, with a .22 rifle nearby. And the little dog came strutting up the drive looking at him in that supercilious, canine manner, or at least in his drunken state he convinced himself it was.

So he took the gun and shot the dog dead.

I'm not sure what he told my mother, who was a young girl at the time, about it. I asked her about it later, and she didn't remember. But he spent the rest of his life regretting doing it, that's for sure.

Another time, and for some reason I believe this was in Brownville, he had a hog. Now when you kill a hog in the fall it's a huge undertaking to get it put away. First you bleed it, then you dress it, and then you brine most of it, after butchering, to put in a barrel. You also render some of the fat to make lard, and season and smoke some bacon.

Well, Coker had been drinking one day—he's the one who told me this—and he decided it was time to kill that hog. This was early in the season, and not really time to butcher a hog. But he decided to do so. He went ahead and slaughtered the animal, then attempted to get help. Dressing a hog usually requires several people dividing the work. It's often a big social event in the country, something neighbors plan ahead for and look forward to. I think that my grandfather wanted this to happen. He wanted to be happy, to have people gather around socializing, and, being drunk, he convinced himself he was going to bring this about.

But, as with most drunken plans, this one went badly awry. Nobody wanted to help him. It was the middle of the day, the middle of the week, and no one had made any plans go over to Coker's and help him put his hog away. So, as he told it to me, he spent the next two days cursing and getting the hog squared away, and ruining a lot of it in the process. By the time he was done, he was wholly miserable. And quite sober.

Coker was never averse to making himself the brunt of his stories. The point was not to portray himself heroically, but to tell a good tale. That was another thing I learned from him.

Coker always had two cars. One was my grandmother's car and one was his. He worked on his to the point where the engine ran as near to silently as one could get. I mean it sounded like electric cars do these days. Like a golf cart. You could not hear the engine running when he was idling at a stoplight, for instance. That old Chevy of his was a wonder. And whenever I or my father had car trouble, we could count on Coker to help fix it (although my dad was no slouch when it came to such things).

Coker had a big tool chest where he kept all manner of automotive tools and gardening implements. As I said, he was also a great gardener. He grew enormous tomatoes that were incredibly succulent. These were his favorite snack. He would sit and cut up one of these tomatoes with his always razor-sharp pocket knife and eat the slices on a summer day.

He was also a great gardener of okra and beans, all of which my grandmother and great-grandmother cooked and canned. He particularly loved to raise hot peppers, and as they canned those peppers, he relentlessly ate them. Sometimes he would just eat hot peppers right out of the jar while we sat and talked.

He liked seafood, oysters especially, as I recall, but I think his favorite food was chicken and dumplings. I remember my grandmother and great-grandmother making batches and batches of it.

As a city man for most of his adult life, Coker missed hunting, I know, and tried to go when he could when he was older. The trouble was he didn't have a rifle after a certain point. He only had a pistol. I still have his .45, a 1911 Colt Commander.

He would go squirrel hunting with his pistol when he could. He also liked to surf fish in the ocean. That was the only time I ever saw him fishing. The truth was that Coker had to work most of the time, and at odd hours, at Sloss and U.S. Steel. But he died with an Alabama fishing license in his wallet, and a permission slip to hunt on some wooded land that I believe was near Tuscaloosa. I think these were talismans for him. Also in the wallet was Revis's phone number, and the phone number of the USW union hall.

Coker Montgomery spent the years of World War II working in the mines, principally the Sayreton Mines. He was classified as an essential worker and could not be drafted. I wondered how he felt about this, and I once asked him if he wish he had gone overseas. He looked at me funny and answered, "Hell no! I didn't want to go over there with them poor fellows. There was a war on; you could get your ass shot off."

In so many ways, Coker was a modern man, a man without

aristocratic Southern pretentions about life. He may have yearned for the country and country ways at times, but he was thoroughly an urban man, and a man of the industrial and electric age.

I believe that, after he retired, he planned to do all the recreational activities that he had given up in order to work. He had bought a camper and was preparing to travel around with my grandmother. But, unfortunately, his heart would not let him. The little clump of nerves that controls the beating rate in his heart muscle gave up the ghost. There was general deterioration in the heart proper as well. They tried many things, and he survived a few years, but he was always weakened after that, and couldn't do the things he wanted, whether it was to travel to Florida or elsewhere. The travel trailer he'd bought stood in the next-door lot for several years unused, until I think he finally sold it not long before he died. Coker lived a hardscrabble life, a lot of it brought on by his own actions, and died too young, I think. I wish my kids could've known him.

For all of my youth, Granddaddy, Memaw, and Mama Cooley lived in a house near the Birmingham airport. The address was 5418 67th Street N. The area is now a green safety zone within the airport boundary. It was slightly west of where 12th Ave N intersects East Lake Boulevard presently.

When I say near, I mean practically *at* the Birmingham airport. This house was directly under the flight path of the big jets as they came in to land. You would be sitting there watching television, say, and a jet would come over and the rumble of its engine would completely drown out the television. The house would shake. The jet roar would drown out any conversation you might be having. You could not even shout and be heard. It would drown out your own thoughts as the big jet came over, and you would have to wait until the thing landed to begin thinking again.

If you were outside it could seem like they were about to hit you, they were so low. The house was literally about a quarter of a mile from the runway. Next door to the house was another house that had been built entirely out of slag from the iron foundries. This substance was the remains of iron ore rock after the ore had been gotten out of it.

So someone had built an entire house out of slag. You see them across the South, these slag houses. The stone is a little like pumice in consistency, but heavier. Anyway, for a while the man next door was a mechanic named Carl Toney who had a small garage he'd built out of sheet-metal next to the slag house. Our family always called it the "rock house," actually.

This guy eventually moved away, and my grandfather rented the garage from him so that he could use it for his own mechanic work. Eventually he rented the whole property and put a garden in the side yard of the rock house, between his house and that one. The rock house had a septic tank, and the garden my grandfather grew was directly over the leach field of that septic tank. His tomatoes grew like crazy in the vicinity of that old tank. So that was one of my grandfather's secrets, how he grew such amazing tomatoes.

My grandfather eventually rented the place, as I said, and my aunt Janice lived in it for a time with my cousin Chris after she was divorced. As for the airport house, finally, with a little political agitation from my mother, the Birmingham Airport Authority bought the whole street out. They did this in order to demolish the houses and make a security strip for the airplanes to fly across as they neared the runway.

Maybe I should say something about my grandfather's bigotry. He was without a doubt prejudiced against black people, and didn't hesitate to say so. Yet, I don't think he ever met a black person he didn't like once he got to know them. His bigotry didn't have much to do with his character.

One thing that he was very serious about was being in a workers union. He was a union man start to finish. He belonged to the mine workers while in the mines, and United Steelworkers #12014 while working in the mills. He told me that the union had saved his job, and possibly his life, at the steel mill once. There were diesel locomotives that they used to move heavy items in the yard. One had caught fire and burned. He believed he may have wired something in the engine incorrectly, and that this led to the fire. The thing burned up, costing thousands of dollars. But the union stood behind him and would not let him be fired over this. He was deeply grateful for this for the rest of his life.

I think a lot of his job was pretty boring and was mostly about sitting around waiting for something to come up, some problem to need troubleshooting. I think also that he drank a lot at work for a couple of years. He told me that he did, in fact. There was a waste pond near the Sloss furnace, for instance, where he used to sit and drink at lunch, drink a whole six-pack of beer, and throw the cans into the waste pond, watching them sink. That's enough beer to pickle one's liver pretty well.

But then in the late 1950s, Louise told him that she had had enough of this. She told him that if he didn't stop drinking she would divorce him. She very clearly meant it, too. Coker was a married man at heart. A family man in every way. This would've meant the end for him, and he knew it. He knew he'd never get a girl like Louise Cooley again. He'd also had the scare of losing his job after the burning locomotive engine at work.

So he quit. He quit cold turkey and he never went back to it. Everyone is astounded by this feat to this day. And the entire time I knew him, he never drank. I never knew the Coker that my mother grew up with, the man who came stumbling home in the early hours of the morning and couldn't quite make it in, but collapsed on the front porch. The guy that she had to step over in order to get to school. And the man who occasionally did random horrible things such as shooting her dog. I don't think he ever raised a hand to her or to Louise, however. Neither one of them would've taken any of that. I think he was a sloppy, incoherent drunk, and was an embarrassment in many ways when he was drinking. But as my mother always said, he wasn't mean. Uncle Jimmy was the mean one when he was drunk. (And, as I've mentioned, kind and gentlemanly—and dapper—when sober, which is the only way I ever knew him.)

So if Coker was an alcoholic, he was a functional alcoholic. He worked every day. He raised his two daughters and supported his family. And by the time I knew him, he was a wonderful man.

My father held him in great regard and always called him "Mister Montgomery" as a term of respect, and, eventually, love. In fact, when Daddy recounted a story about Coker and his tomatoes—well, that was one of the few times I ever saw my father tear up over anything.

Coker was extremely helpful and always there for his daughter Janice, especially when Janice began having troubles from her soon to be ex-husband Robert, who seemed to be a low-level wise guy in a Birmingham crime syndicate, at least back then.

He was always helpful to my mother and my father as well, always there to lend a hand if they needed aid moving or if my father needed some help building or repairing something. He was likewise always at my grandmother's beck and call when it came to household chores. There were few things Coker couldn't fix.

One thing Coker did like to do for himself, however, was to take long weekends and return to Tuscaloosa County to visit his cousins. I don't know what cousins he visited when he went down there. He never took my grandmother down there, or she didn't want to go.

My mother has periodically told me that Coker had an illegitimate child, perhaps a daughter. Maybe that had something to do with his trips to Tuscaloosa County. Maybe not. I don't know, and she herself never knew any of the details about the matter, at least any that she ever told me. And I did ask, of course. Perhaps my grandmother knew. It would be hard to keep anything from my grandmother. She relentlessly ferreted out whatever she wanted to know, or figured out the answer if no one would tell her.

One thing Granddaddy always liked to do with the whole family was return to Tabernacle Baptist Church down in Tuscaloosa County for the annual homecoming. He would also re-decorate the graves there on Decoration Day once a year. He always felt bad about his mother and father not having proper gravestones when I was very young, and he and my father eventually put the gravestones in themselves. I was with them when they did it.

I think my father had the grave markers made, and then the two of them took them to the graveyard, and, after putting in concrete foundations, laid the gravestones for Lizzie Skelton, Taylor Montgomery, and Frances Skelton. All were missing or inadequate for several years before. I'm not sure why Baines and Maria did not have stones made for Fannie Montgomery, or for Taylor. Maria was living abroad a great deal at the time—she and Gene spent years in the wilds of Indonesia as Gene searched for oil for Exxon—and Baines lived in Wisconsin. Revis was in Kentucky. There was just my grandfather nearby. Anyway, one day we all went down to Tabernacle graveyard and put the gravestones in.

My grandfather himself was not buried at Tabernacle. That is another story that I think Coker would've liked. The family graveyard for the Barrons and the Cooleys, but particularly the Barrons—my great-grandmother's maiden name—is at Mount Olive Baptist Church northwest of Birmingham. That is where Coker is buried. This is because he knew that Louise wanted to be buried there, and he didn't really care where he was going to be laid to rest. He told me this.

I was there at the funeral and gave the eulogy. It's one of the better things I've written, I think. Unfortunately, it was hand-written, and I no longer possess it. After that, we went to the Mount Olive graveyard for the burial. The problem was that they had opened up the wrong grave.

Coker and Louise had prepurchased several plots, including plots for my aunt and my mother. My mother has many times laid down on her plot and shown me where she was planning to be buried, by the way. As we approached, my aunt Janice reached over and grabbed my arm and said, "that's my grave."

I thought she was being spooky or dramatic for moment, and I answered noncommittally. "What?"

"That's my grave, Tony," said Janice. "That's the grave where I'm supposed to be buried, and Daddy's is over there." She pointed to where his grave was supposed to be. It had not been dug up. They had gotten the wrong hole open. Well my grandmother was not having any of it. She went and talked to the man who ran the graveyard immediately, then to the undertaker, and eventually they all spoke together. They decided that they would lower my grandfather into the sealed crypt that was at the bottom of this grave, Janice's grave. They would lower the casket, close up the crypt, and then, using a backhoe and a cable, lift it out and take it to the spot where the other grave should be, the spot where it would be buried for good.

They laughed, everyone but me and my grandmother. We stayed until they had dug the other grave with the backhoe. The last I saw of my grandfather, he was in that crypt, in that concrete tomb, dangling from the end of a steel cable as the backhoe tractor trundled across the Mount Olive Cemetery, taking him to his final resting place. It was only then that my grandmother agreed that we could leave.

This is a story Coker Montgomery would have loved to tell on himself. Wish he could have.

Louise

Dorothy Louise Cooley Montgomery (1923-2012)

My great-grandmother Electa Cordelia Barron Cooley named my grandmother Dorothy Louise. I never found out where she got the "Dorothy" from. The "Louise" probably came from Electa's grandmother's name, "Louvisa." People called Louvisa Barron "Lou," but they also called her "Louvissey," which sounds a lot like "Louise." "Dorothy" I don't see in the Barron or Gunter family tree anywhere. Later, my mother was named Martha, which I think was after Electa's mother, Martha Sylvania Gunter Barron, who went by Martha, for the most part. When she was younger she went by Sylvanney Gunter in one early census. But her obituary is for Martha S. Barron.

Dorothy Louise Cooley was born in 1923 in Brookside, Alabama, the year before her own father died. She never knew him. During that next horrible year and the next, my great-grandmother Electa lost her son (or sons, I'm not sure how many, but I've heard, at different times, it was up to three), as well as her husband, Charlie. Others died in her own family, including her older brother, Julius Terry Barron, who passed away two months before her husband in April 1924. Her mother-in-law Helen Cooley died later that year in October.

It must've been horrible for Electa, who was all of twenty-one at the time. Her husband, Charles Martin Cooley (1898-1924) died in a tuberculosis sanitarium. He was there because he'd been hit by a gruesome attack of mustard gas in World War I. He never recovered from what it did to his lungs. He may have contracted tuberculosis later, and, his lungs, already shredded inside, succumbed to it after an extended struggle, marked by those visits to the sanitarium.

By 1925, it was just Electa and Louise having to survive on a meager widow's pension from the Army, I believe, and whatever other income Electa could find. I'm not sure what she was doing while Louise was growing up. By 1932, they were living in Brookside, a coal mining village north of Birmingham, Alabama, probably to be near and receive some help from Charlie's brothers, or her own relatives, who worked there. Charlie's brothers were all coal miners at the time, and I think that she was close to Jesse. In fact, Jesse married Electa's sister, Louannie Barron, in 1925, the year after Charlie died.

Jesse and Louannie eventually moved to northern Indiana to work in the steel mills there, and had a son. Jesse's half-brother Homer also moved there. So there is a branch of both the Cooley and Barron families in the Gary and East Chicago area.

My mother told me that Electa and Louise had their own house at Brookside. My grandmother, Dorothy Louise (I think they might have called her the double name back then), went to Mount Olive Elementary School. I know this because Louise sent in a little paragraph to the *Birmingham News* "Children's Page" that the paper printed. In the short letter, nine-year-old Louise talked about her friends, her dolls, and her kitten, which was named Baby. It is a charming little essay.

> Dear Miss Youngblood: I am a little girl 9 years old. I go to Mt. Olive School. I am in the third grade. My teacher's name is Miss Sarah Jones. I like her very much. My playmates are Frankie Fambrough, Mabel Downs and Lola Mae McPherson. My pastime is playing with my four dolls and my pet cat, named Baby. I hope to see my letter on the Children's Page. DOROTHY LOUISE COOLEY.

Louise was what you might call a firecracker, an explosive, fun-loving personality, a little given to excess, but also full of kindness and love. Coker married her fairly young; I think she was sixteen. Louise was not in the least filled with naïve illusions about life then or ever. I believe that she soon got a job as a secretary at an insurance company in Birmingham, and worked for an income until she was in her sixties. This was made possible by the fact that her mother, Electa Cooley, stayed home with Louise's children.

I think that, even if Louise did grow up in relative poverty, she must've been an extraordinarily cared for and loved child. She was an only child, and there is no doubt Mama Cooley doted on her in every way. Yet there was a shrewdness and intelligence to Louise that never let her sink into sheer self-indulgence, even if she was a bit selfish at times. When she wanted something done, she would remind you of it with a stream of mentions until it got completed. I think this must've worked quite well on her mother. It certainly worked fine on my father and me. Coker slowly but surely caved every time, as well.

Louise had an artistic temperament, and native ability. In later years, she developed the hobby of creating ceramic statuettes and house knickknacks. She eventually made her ceramics work into a part-time business. She bought a kiln and many ceramic molds for forming the decorative statues, bookends, and lamp bases she made. She painted and fired these things and, in the end, they came out looking magnificent. She had wild ducks that looked very lifelike, for instance. The coloration of the brown, black, and off-white paint was really perfect. These creations emerged from the kiln greenish white. The outer beauty then added was all due to her talent. She sold these ceramic knickknacks out of the beauty shop that she'd established in the garage in the yard of the house near the Birmingham airport.

I don't know how she got started as a beautician. I never heard the story. But sometime in the 1950s or early 60s she must have gotten her license and become a full-time hairdresser. She was an expert at producing the kind of hairdos that were in fashion during those times. These were huge piled-up beehives that were teased out to perfection and held in place by half a bottle of hairspray. Through the years, women who elected to keep that hairstyle remained as Louise's customers. She was expert at producing the look they desired. Wherever she worked, her clients followed her. I remember the nice little shop she owned in Tarrant City, a Birmingham suburb. I don't know why she gave that up, but it was probably because the rent was too high or Janice didn't want to do it anymore. In any case, Coker later built her a shop out of a portion of the garage at their house near the Birmingham airport. She used this for years and had many customers come by. They parked in her driveway. She never totally retired until the airport bought them out and they moved. From that settlement, they got a house in Centerpoint, further to the northeast and more suburban, where Coker ended his days.

After Coker died, my great-grandmother Electa began to seriously decline. At this point, it was in the early 1990s, my mother moved back from Dallas, Texas to Birmingham to live with Louise and Electa for nearly three years. She and my father had moved to Texas in 1982, when my father took a job with Hunt Oil as a cartographer. My mother had gotten a job as a mortgage agent in north Dallas. Back in Alabama, she found a job doing some sort of financial work for a bank in Birmingham. After she returned to Dallas, she got positions in mortgage underwriting. She moved around to various companies, but made at least $20-$30,000 more than my father per year for the rest of their working lives. She'd always had to scramble around in Anniston to make a living, mostly selling real estate or assistant managing a small department store. But once she got to Dallas, opportunities bloomed.

Anyway, Mama Cooley had begun to experience dementia, and was in failing health by the end of the 1980s. One of my grandfather's final ailments was a bad back he'd acquired by catching Mama Cooley once when she'd fainted. After that, his back was never the same, hurting him almost as badly as his heart ailments toward the end. He told me he sometimes wished he hadn't caught her, that she may have been all right, but his back certainly never was again. But, of course, he would've done it again if he'd had to.

Mama Cooley had extremely swollen legs. This was edema, a buildup of limbic fluid that caused particularly her lower legs and feet to swell. My grandmother had it and my mother suffers from it terribly in her old age. But otherwise Electa and Louise were remarkably resilient, both living to ninety. It was only in the last five years or so of each of their lives that they experienced decline in mental sharpness, and it wasn't nearly as terrible as the Alzheimer's decline I saw in my father and paternal grandfather. Nevertheless, there is a Alzheimer's allele that I've inherited from my mother's side of the family, so they had at least one Alzheimer's gene, and this may have contributed to their final mild dementia. I, of course, have both alleles and am at great risk for developing Alzheimer's by the time I'm sixty-five.

Louise was a great one for beautification, for making herself up.

She always had lipstick and eyeliner and mascara on when possible. She and my great-grandmother both went to bed with a regiment of Pond's cream covering their faces and a towel or cap over those bouffant hairdos to keep the cream off the coifs. They looked a bit like sea monsters to me.

As I said, Louise decided not to put up with Coker's drinking habit anymore. She gave him an ultimatum and he stopped. They had quite a few arguments for a while when I was young, and at one point Louise moved away for a whole year to her own apartment. They talked about a divorce, but they both began missing one another and started seeing one another again. I remember Memaw pulling up once and whisking away Coker for a date. In the end, they got back together, and never parted again until Coker died. I really don't know what was going on there, but was relieved as a child when it was over.

Louise had blue eyes. My mother's eyes are green. Electa's eyes were, I believe, brown. Charlie Cooley had brown eyes, a ruddy complexion, and was 5'8", according to his World War I draft card, the same height as I am. So Electa and Charlie must have both had a blue iris color allele.

My mother was effectively raised by both of those women, Electa and Louise. She called Louise "Mother" and she called her grandmother "Mama." Electa was always home and was generally the housekeeper. Louise was usually out working days, but home at night. So Martha was surrounded by these women and lived in the cradle of their love.

Louise had Martha in 1941. She and Coker did not have another child until Janice came along six years later. What happened in between was World War II, of course. They probably didn't want to bring a baby into that uncertain time.

After Coker died, Louise had three serious relationships. She got heavily involved with two men whose last names I cannot accurately remember. I believe they were called W.D. and Van. Neither married her because they kept dying. She stayed by both men's side as a girlfriend while they kicked the bucket.

After that, she did remarry. She married a fellow named Jim Poe. Jim was a tall man with a good shock of hair who had probably been rather good-looking in his younger days. He'd been a truck driver for most of his life. He was not exactly the brightest lightbulb in the house.

He was nice enough, but he also developed heart problems and, perhaps, cancer. Louise stayed by his side until he died.

After Jim Poe passed away, she moved in with my aunt. She and Jim had bought a house together in Centerpoint. After Jim died, she sold this and settled in with Janice, who was also living in the same neighborhood. Or perhaps they bought a house together. In any case, this is where my cousin, Christopher Scott England, spent his final teenage years.

And that is how she spent the rest of her life. After graduation, Chris moved down to Mobile, where he went to the University of South Alabama. It took him a while, but I believe he eventually finished a degree there a decade or so later, with lots of time between working at various jobs, and moving back and forth between Mobile and Birmingham.

After Louise had lived with Janice a couple of years, Chris invited them to move down so that he could perhaps live with them in a house. So they moved to Mobile for several years, and Chris did live with them there. But my grandmother and Janice ended up pining for North Alabama. They did not really like Mobile much, or the neighborhood they ended up in. Also it was difficult to live with a young man in thirties who rather enjoyed a life of partying.

Chris, by the way, had trouble saying "Memaw" when he was little, and always called Louise "Ma A," as in the letter "A." He also called his great-grandmother "Coo," not "Mama Cooley," as David and I did.

They moved back north. Janice found a house for them in Gadsden, just up Interstate 59 from the area where they'd lived for so long in northeast Birmingham. It was a pleasant, somewhat ill-formed older house in a southeastern Gadsden lower middle class suburb not far from Noccalula Falls. That is where Louise ended her days, caring for a couple of dogs and a cat. I think the cat she had at the end was called Baby, just like the cat she'd had at nine years old.

Janice called me when Louise was in her final decline, and I drove down from where I lived in North Carolina. When I got there, I found Janice exhausted from caring for her mother. Louise was out of it, mostly unconscious. We took turns sitting with her, and both Janice and I were together, with me holding Louise's hand, as she struggled for breath late one night and, with a final rattling exhalation, expired. I felt her hand grip slacken in my own and knew she was gone.

Louise was such a vital force, such a vivacious personality. It was sometimes a little wearying to be around her energy, especially when you were in a different mood. But the truth was, she always picked me up when I was with her, and, when I was a child, I felt the great love she had for me.

Despite the fact that she worked, she and my great-grandmother were very careful about housekeeping. They were especially solicitous about keeping up the appearance of their yard. My grandmother loved lawn ornamentation. She put things out there, a lot of things. She had concrete flamingos. She had a concrete rabbit that I sat on and rode like a horse when I was a toddler. She had bird baths always, with a little skim of water in them so the birds would come and play.

The two women loved a plant called elephant ear. It had huge green leaves on green stalks rising from the ground. She and Electa also particularly loved to grow hydrangeas, which they called snowball plants, and touch-me-nots. They spent a lot of time working in, and caring for, their yard wherever they lived. At the house by the airport there was a good bit of property attached. Louise at one point cajoled my grandfather into building her a patio. He put down a bunch of bricks and eventually set his swing on it. They had this remarkably springy iron patio furniture. These were chairs made of double-curved slats of steel that you could bounce up and down and rock back and forth. My grandfather often sat in the swing and burned oily shop rags to create smoke to keep the mosquitoes away—away from my grandmother and great-grandmother. He claimed the mosquitoes seldom bothered him.

Louise smoked for many years, but gave it up in the 1970s and never went back to it. This was in contrast to Coker, who could never quit and didn't want to. My great-grandmother never smoked, as far as I know. I never saw a cigarette in her hand, that's for sure.

Louise liked to wear necklaces and jewelry, and had a jewelry collection. So did Mama Cooley. Louise always painted her nails and kept her toenails polished, as well. She was fairly light complexioned, and had been blonde as a child, I believe. I think Janice got her complexion from Louise, and my mother got hers from Coker.

Louise was not a tall woman. She was about my mother's height, around five-foot-four inches. Electa was a bit taller than her, probably five six or seven. Both suffered from arthritis at times, and edema, the limbic fluid build-up in their calves, but otherwise seemed resilient until the very end.

Louise had strong teeth and never got dentures. I know that my great-grandmother for most of her life tried to hide the fact that she had dentures. But when you went into the bathrooms of their houses, there were always the accoutrements of denture cleaning. I frequently saw my grandfather without his teeth in. My great-grandmother tried to keep hers in at all times, even until the end. I can only imagine how annoying the whole regimen of taking care of these must have been for them, the putting in and taking out of dentures. I'm grateful to have all my teeth.

After her own retirement, and my grandfather's death, Louise took up country music line dancing. She attended many senior events, where she dressed in flamboyant outfits. It was during her line dancing period that she met Jim Poe. She really enjoyed going out and being socially engaged. The beauty shop, ceramics, and her other activities had given her that for years. She needed something to replace it. My great-grandmother, on the other hand, was a homebody and never seemed to long for the company of anyone other than her family.

Louise had an accent throughout her life that was very Birmingham lower middle class. It reflected her upbringing in Mount Olive, and the general coal mining district north of Birmingham. She spent most of her life in the city itself, however. They lived in North Birmingham for many years at 1816 34th Ave N in what used to be called the ACIPCO District. ACIPCO is an acronym for American Cast Iron and Pipe, the company that had a huge foundry nearby. Martha attended Phillips High School downtown, where she was an excellent student and very active. It was only in later years that Louise and Coker moved to the east side of town. I think my grandfather just wanted a bit of land, a larger yard, and that area they acquired by the airport was probably dirt cheap, as well.

The house by the airport was a boxy affair. It had three small bedrooms, a living room, and a kitchen. It had to have been less than 1,500 square feet. But it also had that outbuilding my grandfather built. He called it the garage, but he had a closed-in room there, and my grandmother had her shop in part of it, as well. The yard was fairly large for such a place. It must've all seemed very expansive after living in close quarters for years in tightly packed North Birmingham. It was, as I've mentioned, directly—and I mean *directly*—in line with the Birmingham Airport runway, and under take-off and landing paths.

In 1943, Coker lived at 2529 34th Ave N in Birmingham. I believe this was a house they occupied throughout World War II. During the war, Coker's half-sister Maria Montgomery came to live with them for a while. My mother remembers her well from that period. Her name was pronounced Ma-RAI-uh by her parents and my mother. She eventually changed it to the more common pronunciation of Maria, conventional for the twentieth century, after she left the South. Maria worked in an ammunition factory in, I think, Bessemer, Alabama, she later told me, measuring and performing quality control on the size of the shells.

Living with the family in North Birmingham, she probably got to know her big brother Coker far better than she had before. She was nearly fifteen years younger. She would later go on to the University of Alabama and to marry Gene Bottoms. She ended up traveling the world with Gene as the wife of a petroleum geologist, and later as a geological librarian herself. Maria was beautiful when she was young, and my grandmother was herself pretty hot. Louise never saw a camera she didn't like, but she once said to my mother that she did not believe she herself to be pretty, but ugly. I think her hunger for the camera lens was a way of standing up for herself, and making the world notice despite what she believed about herself. Of course, she was wrong. She was pretty, but in an unusual, exotic way, when she was young, and she married a guy who looked like Humphrey Bogart. They made a handsome couple.

Interestingly, Louise and Maria were the same age, born in 1923. My great-grandmother was once a winsome beauty herself, and she was not that old at the time, only in her late thirties. It must've been quite something for Coker to have those three lookers living together in his house at one time.

One propensity Louise did have was to occasionally choke on food going down. It got stuck in her esophagus, not her windpipe. I inherited this from her, and it was an ailment that bothered me particularly in my twenties and thirties. I think she and I both also suffered from the acid reflux related ailment that I've had for many years. She drank a lot of milk, and that seemed to soothe her stomach.

So did my great-grandmother. My mother was long an aficionado of buttermilk.

Dorothy Louise Cooley Montgomery led a successful life. She raised her two daughters, worked busily for years, and enjoyed herself. She skated by on her wit and intelligence a great deal, as well as her looks and her ability to manipulate others. Yet she did start two successful small businesses, and ended up with a bunch of people who loved her greatly at the end.

Below is the eulogy and remembrance I delivered at her funeral.

⋅→⟫⊜⟪←⋅

Dorothy Louise Cooley was born April 6, 1923, in Brookside, Alabama. Her father was Charles Martin Cooley, who had served in the first World War and been gassed. Charles Cooley's respiratory system probably never recovered from that experience and he died young, soon after Louise was born. Within the space of two years, Louise also lost her brother (or brothers), leaving only herself and her mother, Lecter Cooley, to carry on together. Carry on they did, and Lecter Cooley, Mama Cooley to me, lived with Louise for the remainder of her life.

In the late 1930s, Louise met James Coker Montgomery, who had left the company town of Brownville outside of Tuscaloosa and moved to Birmingham where he worked as an electrician in the coal mines of North Birmingham, and later as an electrician for U.S. Steel and others in the Birmingham foundries, including his last job, which was at Sloss Furnace. Coker and Louise set up shop with Mama Cooley, and soon daughters Martha Ann and Janice were born. They lived in North Birmingham, Woodlawn, at one time made a try at living in the country, then moved back and eventually settled in a house near the Birmingham airport for many years—a house and yard I remember fondly from my childhood.

Louise Montgomery became "Memaw" when I came along, a tradition carried on by my brother David, and then also became known as "Ma A," with the coming of my cousin Chris. For my mother, Martha, and my Aunt Janice, she was always "Mother."

The first thing that comes to mind when anyone thinks of

Memaw is the phrase "full of life." Memaw was not a timid woman. She was a go-getter, someone determined to live her life to the fullest. And she did. Times were hard in the late 1930s, and they didn't get much easier in the coming decade. With the support of Mama Cooley at home helping to take care of the girls, Memaw went to work, and she worked hard. She held several jobs over the course of the years, in offices and stores. Finally, she put her love of beauty to work for her, and became a hair stylist for a long span of years. This is what I remember her doing in my youth. She eventually ran her own shop in Tarrant City and North Birmingham.

I have many childhood memories of visiting Memaw in her shop. In fact, I remember well that my brother and I took a proprietary interest in that shop whenever we came around, and we attempted to completely rearrange it to our own liking on several occasions. Memaw endured this disruption with good humor, as she did so many other disruptions in her life. She understood that a shop can be put back in order, but that the misplaced devotion and amusing behavior of a grandchild is a precious matter that must be cherished in the moment. I remember her shaking her head and smiling at David and me, even as she showed just enough irritation to keep us out of her cabinet of scissors and from playing in the blue sanitizing solution.

Here is another word that springs to mind when I think of Memaw: undaunted. This was a lady undaunted by hardship, undaunted by setbacks in life. Memaw did not believe in defeat or defeatism in the slightest. Oh, she got sad and discouraged at times, but she soon determined to spring back, and spring back she did. And when Memaw got a notion to do something, that thing usually got done, one way or another. I remember her driving her Corvair all over town when I was young. I think Memaw began to drive while quite young, and against any resistance from others. Memaw took pride in her driving, and the independence it gave her. She was proud of teaching both daughters to drive, as well.

Memaw's undaunted attitude included me, especially during my college years, after granddaddy began having heart trouble, and the grass needed cutting at the house by the airport. I might object that my studies at Birmingham-Southern were very difficult and I must be left to my books, but this cut no sauce with Memaw. She would listen to my complaints and answer sedately: "Uh huh. Tony, I want you to cut the grass. It really needs it, and Coker can't do it no more."

Many will testify to this feisty nature in Memaw. Yet while Memaw was utterly determined to make the most of what she had, and to get you to do *your* part, as well, she always handled it all with a big dollop of love.

There was never a moment of doubt in my heart that Memaw loved me dearly. It helped that she told me so all the time.

Grace and love. Two more words that describe Memaw. Because while Memaw was a woman out in the world doing things of the world, there was also a deep spiritual side to her nature. She was a Christian, of course, and eventually a dedicated member of the Assembly of God, including with the big church in Centerpoint, Huffman Assembly of God, where I have many childhood memories of attending services with her and of the joy she took in the music, the singing, and in listening to the preaching of the Word of God in a robust fashion by the preachers there.

And another phrase that describes Memaw's nature, a phrase that is very important to me because I became a writer and I'm in the arts and letters by profession, is love of beauty. Memaw loved her yard, and took care of it. She loved her plants and flowers, from the gardenias to her elephant ears and more. She loved her bird baths filled with jays and sparrows, and her kettle pot planters full of pansies.

Memaw was an artist in her work and in her life. In her sixties, she became an expert at creating ceramics and made gorgeous porcelain and ceramic figures that she painted in completely life-like manner and fired in her own kiln. In fact, Memaw became so good at ceramics that she taught it for a while. I have some of her figurines and am still amazed at the colors she got into them, how she transformed them from mere ornaments to objects of beauty.

She also applied her love of beauty to her own appearance. Here is another word for Memaw: vivacious. Full of life and spirit. Memaw loved to dress up. She loved her makeup. She loved to pick out her clothes and shoes and adornment and go out into the world in style. In her later years, she was a line dancer, and, after granddaddy died, she acquired a second husband, Jim Poe, in the process, from among her dance crowd. Jim, like Coker before him, was a handsome man who kept up a good appearance. Memaw liked men who took care of themselves and worried a bit about their looks. This was part of her artistic nature, as well, I believe.

Most of all, when I think of Memaw, the word that comes up most is love. Memaw loved me. She loved her daughters, her grandsons, her great-grandchildren. She loved both husbands, and her love for her husband Coker, who was, I think it goes without saying, the big love of her life, was deep and abiding and a commitment through thick and thin. There were some very hard times, and my grandfather was not always an easy man to live with, although he was always a loving man by and large, and there was no doubt that, whatever arguments the two might be having, this was a love match.

A life force, and a force of nature. That is maybe the best description of Memaw of all. Now Memaw is gone from this world, and it is as if a force of nature has passed through, a life-force hurricane of love and activity. For so long, Memaw was a given in our lives, and now those winds might seem to have quieted. Some people pass through this world with nary a peep. Not Memaw. She was life writ large, and she left a mark. The question for us is what do we do now?

I think the answer is to not change a thing. We need to remember that life force of Memaw and determine that we ought to go at life with just such love and push and passion ourselves. I think Memaw would expect it of us. This was a woman who made sure she was in any picture that was being taken around her, made sure her opinion was known in any discussion, made sure that nobody took advantage of her daughters and mother, and that all respect was given to her and those she loved.

I imagine heaven a little differently than most, perhaps. I don't know about golden harps and angel wings and such. Those are familiar images for things we cannot possibly understand. I think heaven is perhaps like an awakening into a world that is more real than real. That this world is but a shadow compared to the world God has prepared for us hereafter.

And I believe in my heart that Memaw is in that world now, in that world that is more real than real. That she is doing all the things she loved, creating beauty, living life to the fullest, in some incomprehensible, greater way than we can even imagine. That those she loves surround her. I also feel that the beauty we see—in nature, in others—is now a reflection of a love greater than all loves which Memaw will forever have a hand in creating.

→⊸▬◉◖═⊷←

The Barrons and Cooleys
-‹›⸺◉⸺‹›-
Mama Cooley

Electa Cordelia Barron Cooley (1903-1994)

Electa Cordelia Barron was born in Blount County, somewhere around Oneonta, Alabama, I think. She called herself, and most people called her, "Lecter," or "Lecta." Yet my mother insisted that her name was actually "Electa," and Mama Cooley went along with this for most of her life.

She was the daughter of Luther Barto Barron and Martha Sylvania Gunter. The Barrons and the Gunters went three generations back in that part of Alabama. The Barrons had originally come over from Georgia, where they were previously a well-to-do family that had fallen on hard times after the Civil War.

I don't know a great deal about Electa's upbringing, but I do know that she lived in a house full of girls. There was one older brother already out in the world, and one little brother, born after she moved away. There were six sisters in all. She stayed fairly close to them throughout her life. We particularly visited Aunt Josie and Aunt Mae. The daughters of her sister Mae became the playmates of my mother when they were all young, and Betty Gibb Baker is now one of the last people my mother regularly talks to on the phone in her old age.

It must've been a pretty happy household with all those girls. I hope so, because Mama Cooley went through some very trying times after that. She married Charlie Cooley just after he returned from World War I in June of 1919. He had been gassed by the Germans in Europe, and his lungs were not good after that. Nevertheless, he was otherwise vital, because they had at least one son—and Louise.

I believe that, over the next few years, Charlie either picked up tuberculosis, or his weakened lungs just began to collapse. The record shows that he was checked into the national sanitarium in Tennessee three times for treatment. Each time he spent several months there. The 1920 census shows Electa living at home with her parents. In 1924, Charlie died in that Tennessee sanitarium. His body was returned and buried at Mount Olive Cemetery. This left Electa widowed at twenty-one years of age. She never remarried. She called herself Lecter *Cooley* for the rest of her life.

I know that, in addition to Louise, she had a son, and possibly two or more sons, in that period between 1919 and 1924. There is a picture of Charlie holding a boy who is identified as Charlie Junior. In any case, the child or children all died around the same time as their father, but from some sort of stomach ailments, as my mother told it. But, as my mother also once said, "children just died back then, and nobody knew why." I never got the full story, and I don't believe my mother did either. I can only imagine the devastation Electa must have felt.

One interesting fact is that, when she was young, Louise was made fun of for the way that she pronounced "Mama." I have no idea why this was, or how she said it. Maybe it was that the country accent she picked up from Oneonta didn't translate well to the metropolis of Brookside, or something like that. In any case, she stopped calling my great-grandmother by that name or *any* name. Early on, she had worked out ways to talk to Mama Cooley without using the word "Mama" or "Mother" or "Mom," and there is only one or two times that I ever heard her call Mama Cooley by name. She did use "Mama" at those times, spoken very softly, and I think she regularly called her that when they were alone. It was a pretty amazing thing, and it really struck me as a child how cleverly my grandmother got around calling her own mother anything. It didn't seem to bother Mama Cooley at all. Maybe she'd even encouraged it earlier. I never found out.

When Coker came along and married Louise, he moved in with the two of them, mother and daughter, and lived with them for the rest of his life. Which is not to say Electa didn't get out. When I was a baby and my mother was in Tuscaloosa working and going to the University of Alabama, Electa came over and stayed with us for long stretches. She took care of me, and then David. At one point, she had hurt her arm, or perhaps her leg—I cannot remember now—rather badly, and she told me some years later that rocking me had rebuilt the strength in the extremity.

Mama Cooley I remember as having clear brown eyes. She had fair skin and she kept it pliable with that repeated regime of Pond's cream at night and lotion during the day. I think she was proud of her complexion.

She was indeed quite the young beauty in her early pictures. But she became an old lady in manner, I think, before her time, always identifying as a widow after Charlie died. I think she never went out with another man, or even considered a relationship thereafter.

The basic characteristics of Electa Cooley were her inner calm and her abiding love. Everyone who knew her characterized her as a saint. I think a lot of her family knew what she had been through, as well. To me, she was the perfect maternal, grandmotherly presence. She was always feeding me and taking care of any injuries or other little problems I had as a child. She always had a kind smile and words of encouragement about anything I might want to do. David and I used to argue that there were actually two perfect people born in human history. One was Jesus Christ. The other was Mama Cooley.

One thing that did afflict her—and it was something that afflicted both Louise and my mother—was night terrors. She would wake up in the middle of the night moaning and calling out inarticulately. Usually this was after a dream of a big black dog chasing her, or something like that. This happened to my grandmother as well, and it is still happening to my mother. Periodically you will just hear her moaning in terror in the middle of the night. I hesitate to wake her because if it passes she will not remember whatever this horrible dream might have been, but if she wakes, she will. My grandfather Coker used to comment on Electa's night terrors, how sometimes she shook the house with her moans and cries.

But in general, Electa was an utterly placid presence which calmed down any situation. You did not want to get in to a bad argument in front of her. You never wanted to cause her any upset. She made everyone feel like a better person for being around her.She read fairly regularly, mostly religious books. She did not have any particular interests like my grandmother did, say country music or charismatic religion. She mostly just went along with Louise down whatever path of enthusiasm Louise was traveling. I am pretty sure they grew up Baptist, but Louise found a church in Huffman, the nearby suburb of Birmingham, a large Assembly of God. It was one of the very first mega-churches, and employed an electric band with a country music flavor. It had a well-coiffed pastor named Dan Ronsivalle. Both my grandmother and great-grandmother liked their men with nice, thick hair, preferably worn brushed back and high.

Huffman Assembly was a charismatic evangelical church. They attempted physical healing by prayer. They spoke in tongues and interpreted that seeming babble by divine gift. They believed in all of the gifts of the spirit that are spoken of in *Acts*, and that, apparently, the early Christians experienced.

As for me, I thought it was some of the weirdest stuff I ever saw. Electa and Louise went to an Assembly of God church for the rest of their lives after that, however. I do think that Electa's Christian belief was a great solace and of great importance to her, whatever form it took. And I don't think it much mattered what denomination she chose. She was just happy in church.

Both my grandmother and great-grandmother were quite prejudiced toward black people, but also extremely kind toward any they knew personally. I never saw them do anything mean to anyone. It was just in the way that they talked, the words they used. I think this was why it was fairly easy for my mother to completely dispense with any bigotry or prejudice she might've been brought up with. She doesn't have a trace of this in herself.

For me when I was young, the casual bigotry that came out every once in a while was just a curiosity of my grandparents. I really thought nothing of it other than that it made them seem old-fashioned. The idea that it tainted everything else about them seems ludicrous to me. On the contrary, it seems to me that it affected nothing truly basic about them at all. When people say otherwise, I simply don't argue with them because I think them fools.

The only even slightly aristocratic strain that I've detected in my ancestral lines are the Barrons. They go back to a Georgia family that was quite well-to-do. In fact, until I began my genealogical research, I had no idea about any of that. I grew up convinced that none of my ancestors owned slaves, and, for the most part, that is correct. Almost all were family farmers on all sides, and there were no slaves anywhere to be found.

However, the Barrons did own slaves. Calvin Hamilton Barron (1823-1913), great-grandfather of Electa, was the son of Barnabas Barron (1793-1864) of Hart County, Georgia. Barnabus had 3,000 acres in Hart County. It was good farming country, inland from Savannah.

Barnabas Barron was postmaster of the area, as well. I believe that he married the daughter of one of the rich landholders in the area, too. I don't know where he came from, or how he acquired his land and money to make his start. His sons fought in the Civil War, including my direct ancestor, C.H. Barron. His older son, William B. Barron, was wounded in the leg by a Yankee slug. After suffering a great deal, he died a year later. William Barron's wife passed away soon thereafter, leaving all of their children orphaned.

These Barron children were divided up, and Calvin and his wife, Harriet Wilkinson Barron (1830-1900), took in two of them.

The end of the war seems to have brought an end to the Barron prosperity. Calvin eventually migrated to North Alabama and acquired a farm there, bringing along his son, Rufus Barnabus Barron. Rufus Barney married a woman named Louvisa Caroline Pritchett. Louvisa was from Georgia. I believe that they still lived in Georgia when they met.

Louvisa Barron, everyone said, was extremely dark complexioned. In fact my mother had heard the Barron girls called their grandmother "Black Dutch." In the South, that can mean several things, but in North Alabama it generally refers to American Indian, particularly Cherokee, ancestry. But it can also refer to the belief that there is Moorish blood from Spanish Dutch ancestry flowing in the person's veins.

I believe Louvisa is why we have the rumor of Cherokee ancestors in the family. Maybe she did have a bit of Cherokee blood. Indeed my DNA test shows that there is a 0.3 percent Native American strain in my genetics from somewhere, but I am not entirely convinced by these trace findings in what is a very young science.

One thing my DNA test, and that of my mother, has convinced me of is that people generally had children by the people they were married to, and they usually stayed married until one of the partners died. Reviewing DNA matches, I've found no real surprises, and a whole lot of confirmation of the paper trail. In fact, it is astonishingly consistent.

And the truth is that the records are pretty clear: Louvisa Pritchett's parents were normal Georgia settlers, and not Cherokees. I don't know the truth of the matter, but I do know that my mother believed that somewhere in our ancestry were people who'd been picked up in Dutch-controlled Spain by some English ship coming to the New World in the 1600s, and that Moorish blood had come along for the ride. I don't know where she got this tale. Perhaps it was from the research she did the summer we lived in Washington, D.C., and she was looking into genealogy at the Library of Congress and National Archives.

I believe that they also sometimes called Louvisa Barron "Lu-VI-cie," with a long "i" sound. Perhaps my mother had taken that name, Vice, to be a surname or maiden name, and inferred that it was Dutch. Knowing how dark complexioned Lou Barron was, perhaps Mom concocted this explanation in her mind. I don't know. In any case, there is more than one account of the dark, wide visage of Louvisa Barron.

Rufus Barney was not Louvisa's first husband. She'd had some children before, and was a widow when he married her, I think. Luther Barto was definitely their boy, however. I have no idea where the middle name Barto came from. Obviously, Rufus's middle name came from Barnabas, his grandfather. So the Barrons, the Dooleys, the Pritchetts, and the Wilkinsons were all very much Georgia people. Where they came from beyond that I don't know for certain, but I'm pretty sure Barron is a Scottish name, or perhaps a name from Northern Ireland. Since I am apparently three-quarters descended from Scotch-Irish, as we Southerners call them, I would guess that is where they are from.

One gets the sense that the Barrons had a somewhat aristocratic air, or at least that they did not think of themselves as hard dirt farmers. I don't know how much such an attitude affected Electa. She grew up a long way away from those plantation days of great-great grandfather, Barnabas Barron, that's for sure.

On Electa's mother's side there are many farmers, and also a heritage that stretches back to the early 1600s. Martha Gunter's father had the interesting name of Kinchen Gunter. I believe that was the maiden name of one of his grandmothers. There's a picture of Kinchen and his wife I've seen. He looks like a pleasant and amusing fellow sitting on his porch there. He's bushy-bearded, of course.

The Cooleys

Joshua Wade Cooley (1877-1945)

The Joshua Wade Cooleys are an interesting clan to research. It took me a while to untangle what I believe is the story with Josh Cooley's boys. Josh Cooley, my great-grandfather's father, definitely is the son of John Franklin Cooley of Tennessee. John F. Cooley is another Civil War ancestor of mine. There is a wonderful photo of John in his Civil War uniform as a young man. There are a bunch of DNA hits from other descendants of his that match-up with my mother's DNA. I think I've seen more matches to John Franklin Cooley than anyone, probably due to the fact that his photo is so much out and about on the genealogy portion of the Internet. And he had five wives.

Anyway, it appears to me that Josh Cooley first married a woman name Betty Jenkins. There is a marriage license that indicates this. This greatly puzzled me at first because Josh was married twice more. The woman he was married to while the Cooley boys were teenagers was named Helen Cooley. And in the 1910 census there is also in his house a young man named Claud Jones. He is listed as a stepson. I momentarily thought that Helen must have had the maiden name of Helen Jones. But she was *not* Helen Jones—because she had married a man named Jones, and had Claud Jones with him. In fact, the record was there once I realized I needed to look. Helen married a man named James Jones, who either died or from whom she was divorced, I don't know which. The point is, she was with someone else at the turn of the century.

This is the kind of thing you run into when you are looking into your ancestors and nobody is still alive to lay it all out for you.

The marriage of Josh and Helen Cooley did not take place until 1906. The first three Cooley men, Charlie, Jesse, and Earl, were all born before that. Only Homer was born after. This means that Charlie, Jesse, and Earl were full brothers by another woman, and Homer was their half-brother. It also means that Homer Cooley was Helen's son, and so half-brother to Claud Jones, but the other boys were not. Yet on several forms Charlie Cooley lists his mother as variously Helen Jones or Helen Smith. The fact is, she could not be his biological mother. It had to be Betty Jenkins.

Charlie was clearly not thinking of my needs when he did this!

Earl Cooley acknowledged this later in life when he began listing Betty Jenkins as his mother on various forms. I believe this was after Helen Cooley died. I think all the Cooley boys considered her to be like a mother to them, but they all knew who their biological mother was, as well.

Claud Jones, Helen's other son, was clearly adopted wholesale into the Cooley household, because he was later the bondsman for his half-brother Jesse on his marriage to Louannie Barron, Electa's sister, in March of 1925. A little further research indicates that Helen's maiden name was Smith. So Helen Smith married a guy named Jones. They had a son, Claud James Jones (1898-1956). Claud went on to marry Gertrude Liza Tilley (1907-1991).

Interestingly, Gertrude Tilley's brother Romey enters into the Barron line obliquely. Romey Tilley (1904-1976) had a daughter with Mary Frances Walker Barron (1901-1958), the widowed wife of Julius Terry Barron, Electa's older brother. It's unclear if they married. I don't think so. The daughter, Imogene Verdia Barron (1929-1987), called herself Imogene Barron on most of her records, including her own marriage license. But she couldn't possibly be Julius Terry's biological daughter, since she was born in 1929, five years after Julius Terry died. Others affirm that Romey Tilley is her father, as well.

So the Cooleys and the Barrons were tangled up three different ways. The Cooleys, Barrons, Joneses, and Tilleys must have been living near one another at different times. The Cooleys were coal miners from Tennessee originally, so perhaps they were all connected to North Alabama mines in some way.

One interesting tidbit that I hesitate to mention were it not so striking, is that I have seen a photo of Romey Tilley—and in that photo he is a dead ringer for my grandfather, Coker Montgomery, so much so that I was sure of it for a while. But my mother took a look at the photo and said it was not him. The resemblance is uncanny, however.

Helen Cooley died later in the same year as her stepson, my great-grandfather, Charlie. She was only forty-six. What a calamitous year for the Cooleys and Barrons 1924 was. In 1926, Josh Cooley married for a third time, to Malinda Millikan, who was called Molly. He had no children by her that I know of.

It took me a while to parse together a story on the progeny of the Cooley men. I knew Josh married Helen in 1906. It is extremely unlikely that they were living together before that. People didn't do that. Also Helen, of course, has a marriage record with James Jones, and a son by him, Claud, born in 1898. So it belatedly dawned on me that Helen could not be the first three Cooley boys' mother.

Betty Jenkins must've been from Tennessee, but I haven't found any other real evidence. I've followed one blind trail after another. There are Betty Jenkinses on census forms, but it's impossible to say which is the correct one. So she, at the moment, represents a brick wall in my research. The following is my present best understanding of the situation.

Josh Cooley's Household

Josh Cooley and Betty Jenkins
m. 1896
Children
Charles Martin (*my great-grandfather, married Electa*)
Jesse Lee (*married Electa Barron's sister, Louannie*)
Earl S.

Josh Cooley and Helen Smith
m. 1906
Children
Homer

Helen Smith and James Jones
m. circa 1898

Children
Claud Jones

Josh Cooley and Molly Millikan
m: 1926
Children
None

This is, I think, a prime example of Southern genealogy. It's a puzzle with people attached (the only kind of puzzle I've ever had any interest in solving) and it absorbed my free moments for quite a while. I'm still working at it.

The Cooleys were definitely miners by trade. They all list it in the census and elsewhere. They seem to have moved from Tennessee to Alabama because they found jobs in the mines. I'm sure that before that they were farmers, since practically everybody was. John Franklin Cooley was a farmer, and Josh was likely raised on his farm. John Cooley lived to a ripe old age and was married five times. But the woman who produced Josh was Nancy Ann Lance (1840-1884). Josh is listed in the 1880 census as three years old where she is listed as the female head of household. Nancy is pretty definitely Josh's mom, I'd say. The Lances were actually Lentzes, of German descent. Yikes, this means that I may be somehow related to my own wife, who is a native German!

I wish I knew more about Charles Martin Cooley, my great-grandfather. He died in his twenties. My grandmother never knew him. My great-grandmother revered his memory, but never talked about him. He went into the U.S. Army as a private in Company K of the 4th Alabama Infantry. I'm not sure how he was ultimately deployed in World War I. The 4th Alabama became the 167th Infantry Regiment, and fought in the Second Battle of the Marne, and later performed occupation duty in Germany. Wherever Charlie was, his position put him in place to be hit by poison gas, so I assume he was on or near the front lines. In the next few years, though he married and had children, his tattered lungs couldn't sustain him, and the poor man died in a veteran's sanitarium trying get healthy enough to live what might have been a long life, but was not.

More Montgomerys

Massana Taylor Montgomery (1877-1956)

Coker Montgomery's father's name was Massana Taylor Montgomery. In some family genealogies the "Massana" is turned to "Manassas," but I have a document where he signed Massana. Usually he signed "M. Taylor Montgomery." I don't know where that first name came from. Possibly it is Biblical. His father was a preacher. Massana is a town in Italy and a province of Andorra. Everyone knew him as Taylor, however. He had a maternal ancestor, great-grandmother Mary Margaret Taylor (1794-1848), so maybe the name he went by, Taylor, came from her.

He was, as I've said, a farmer and a woodcutter. His occupation once is listed as "blacksmith," so he was probably good at that trade, as well. He was a great lover of nature, as well. I believe he spent a lot of time out in the woods by himself. My mother remembers particularly that he took her on long walks through the forest on Sundays when she was visiting. He would use his walking stick, which she lovingly preserved, and I still possess. Young Martha loved these walks. They would stroll in the woods as he talked about trees and nature and such. He must've known it all very intimately.

She told me a story about going for a walk with him one time with a little dog, which was following them. The little dog smelled something, then ran over and began to roll in what looked like a pile of leaves. My mother thought this was delightful, but then Taylor Montgomery pointed out that the dog was rolling in a dead animal of some sort.

Despite this one instance, Martha remembers those walks as some of the happiest times in her childhood. I have Taylor Montgomery's walking stick. He must've cut it from a tree in the woodland around Brownville. It was formed by a creeper vine that twirled around a sapling and gave the sapling the shape of the vine. My father later painted and stained it. As with everything my father did when it came to craft, he was careful and thorough. It is a very pretty piece.

My mother remembers Taylor using it on those walks when it was a simple, gray stick, worn from years of use in the woods of Tuscaloosa County. I, too, vaguely recall it from before. It was in our living room for years, and I played with it as a toddler. Sometimes, to my adult chagrin, my brother and I used Taylor's stick as a sword. We also had a dull, old cavalry saber my mother had picked up somewhere, and David and I crossed blades with cane and sword occasionally. As an adult, I've taken it on short trails every once in a while. I think Taylor Montgomery would approve of that. I don't know how he acquired the stick, but I have in my imagination a scene of Taylor Montgomery coming across that vine-encircled sapling while out wood-cutting in the swampland forest around Brownville one day. I envision him stopping, having a look, thinking what an interesting walking cane it would make. I picture him carefully cutting it, taking it home, letting it dry from the green over weeks or months. Sanding it to smoothness (it was always smooth, even before my father lacquered it). Then using it for years and years. It is a beautiful and strange piece, but he made it firstly for walking.

My grandfather for many years had Taylor's hat, which you can see in one of the surviving photos of Taylor. I remember it sitting on the top shelf in Coker's coat closet in the hall of the airport house. It's a big, broad-brimmed black hat, and looks cool. I don't know what became of it, but I wish I still had it, of course.

I don't believe that Taylor Montgomery died owning much more than hat and walking stick, to tell the truth. Maria Montgomery Bottoms (1923-2017) told me years later that, when she said that she wanted to go to Tuscaloosa and attend college, her father gave her his blessing—and a couple of quarters. He said that's all that he could provide for her tuition.

I think he was a loving man and tried to take care of his boys as best he could when his first wife died (she was 38), but in the end had to send them away for their own good. The woman he remarried was interesting, Frances Alvin Skelton Montgomery (1885-1971). My mother was acquainted with Fannie Montgomery quite well and I knew her. I remember her from the nursing home in Tuscaloosa where we visited her fairly often when I was young.

My mother particularly remembers that Fannie Montgomery kept jars full of black widow spiders in her house. She did this because she loved the way that they looked. She thought they were quite pretty. My mother thought this was odd and kind of scary, of course, but she loved Granny, as she called her, and was really the only one who visited Fannie in her old age. Maria had moved far away by that point, and was living in Indonesia, I think, when Fannie Montgomery died. Baines Taylor Montgomery (1925-2008), her son, was living in Madison, Wisconsin. He moved up there after he went to Korea, and never came back to Alabama except to visit. Later, when I was in Wisconsin a few times with a former girlfriend from there, I visited with Baines and had a couple of meals with him at the VFW hall. He was a very nice man, and his wife was sweet, as well. I briefly met a couple of my cousins up there, also.

Baines Montgomery was a tall man, about six feet, I'm pretty sure, and Maria was a fairly tall woman herself. I believe that Taylor Montgomery was tall, too. My mother says he was. Baines had a certain characteristic Montgomery appearance, just as my grandfather did. So did Maria. It is a particular creasing around the lips and the possession of high cheekbones—hard to describe, but easy to see in them.

Uncle Baines had developed a thick Wisconsin accent by the time I met him, which was pretty funny considering the depth of the Alabama country from which he sprang. Maria had completely shed her Alabama accent. My mother never really had one, as far as I know. But both my grandfather and grandmother had pretty extensive Birmingham and Tuscaloosa accents. My paternal grandparents had a distinct Northeast Alabama twang, Emmett especially. He pronounced "fire" and "tire" as "fahr," and "tahr," making them almost two syllables. Myrtice said "furniture" as "FURN-i-chur" and always put the "ch" in "architect." None of these accents is anything like the Southern accent that you see portrayed in many films and such. It is very upcountry, not quite hillbilly, such as a Tennessee or Appalachian accent, but definitely not a drawl, in any sense.

My mother sounds like she could be from anywhere in the Midwest. My father had a slightly more pronounced Southern accent, but not really very noticeable. You wouldn't have been able to place his origins just by listening to him. As for myself, nobody ever suspects that I grew up in Alabama until I tell them.

I pronounce "Tuesday" with the "TY" sound, and "coupon" as "CYEW-pon." I wait *on* the bus, not *for* the bus, but I wait *in* line, and not *on* line, and I have several other Southern usages in my speech. I use y'all a lot now, although I didn't really use it that much growing up (but was aware of how to deploy it even then). I do have an aversion to using "you guys" collectively, as that is Yankee-speak. I have, however, modified the way I say "cool" and "school" in order to be understood by Northern types.

I never use such colloquialisms as "bless your heart" or any other cloying words or idioms that have come into prominence. Those are mostly from South Alabama. In fact, people from South Alabama have a culture distinct from people from North Alabama. South Alabama culture descends from plantations and farming of the extremely rich land. It is quite different from North Alabama culture, which descends from yeoman farmers who participated in almost no slavery to speak of, and did a lot of starving.

On a historical note, that's one of the reasons that I put credit in the idea that the South was fighting for states rights rather than slavery in particular. My North Alabama ancestors didn't own slaves, and didn't know anybody who owned slaves. Their economic system was not built around slavery. One is forced to conclude that all those fellows such as John Franklin Cooley and Hartford Moss Daniel who went to fight had other reasons for doing so. I don't think they cared about defending slavery as an institution. I think that their motivation came from elsewhere. Whether that motivation was equally fallacious, I cannot say. But their reasons for fighting were not economic, or at least not about the ownership of other human beings.

I don't know a great deal more about Taylor Montgomery. Maria told me some. I sat her down once and asked her about her early recollections. I have those recordings. My best insight into Taylor is when my mother once said to me (when I was in my early 50s), "you remind me of him." She was talking about his personality, and I took it as a great compliment.

Taylor Montgomery's father was a preacher, and, I think, was regionally known. He was married to Narcissus Loftis. She looks quite severe in photographs, and I have the feeling that she was probably an imposing presence in real life. Beyond that are Montgomerys that stretch into the Carolinas and to Virginia. They go as far back as the Daniels in my research, and trace to northern Ireland. There was even a Revolutionary Era soldier or two in there on the maternal lines.

What is more easily verified is the migration from the Carolinas to Alabama. I think there was a family group including several Montgomery lines that came down together to Tuscaloosa County from northern Mecklenburg County, where present-day Charlotte, North Carolina, is located. Since William Charles Montgomery was born in Alabama in 1822, and the 1810 census has John in North Carolina, this would have been sometime around 1820, probably a little earlier, say 1818. It appears they stopped for a while in St. Clair County, where William Charles was born, then moved on to Tuscaloosa. John and Margaret Montgomery are established in Tuscaloosa County by the 1850s census. John's father, Robert McCamey Montgomery (1740-1834), is one of our possible Revolutionary War veterans.

John may have been a soldier in the War of 1812. Barnabas Barron, the father of Calvin Hamilton Barron and Electa's great-grandfather, was definitely a soldier in 1812. He also signed a loyalty oath to the United States after the Civil War was over. There's a letter of recommendation endorsing him to receive clemency stating that he was previously a postmaster in the area, and there's record of him having been so. He must've wanted to sign the loyalty oath in order to retain some property or assume an office or do something legal, because otherwise I don't think it was required of everyone.

William Baines Montgomery (1855-1916) is William Charles Montgomery's son, and the father of Taylor Montgomery. This is when the name "Baines" enters into the family, possibly from W.C. Montgomery's short-lived wife, Margaret Dempsey Griffin Montgomery (1825-1859), and his Griffin in-laws. It gets tossed around a bit among later Montgomerys, where "Baines" pops up as a name in a couple of lines.

The Skeltons

Elizabeth Skelton Montgomery (1881-1919)

For a while when I was younger, I knew nothing about Coker Montgomery's mother other than that her name was Lizzie. It took me a while to find out more about Lizzie Skelton because of my confusion of her with Taylor's second wife, Frances Alvin Skelton. At first I didn't quite believe they shared a last name, and that I must have gotten mixed up, but it is so. And it says so on the tombstones in the Tabernacle Church graveyard.

Anyway, Lizzie Skelton's people have left quite a remarkable record, and a record going back a very long way. It's through Lizzie that I think the family has legitimately documented Revolutionary War soldiers, such as Archibald Taylor, and William Holcombe. One strain of Lizzie Skelton's ancestors includes the DePriests, who are apparently of French origin, first coming to America sometime in the 1700s. One of the DePriests, Randolph DePriest (1758-1830), was likely a Revolutionary War soldier, as well. It was Anna DePriest (1782-1849), Randolph's daughter, who married into the Skelton line. Skelton is a very Scottish name, I believe, and I think the family originally comes from a Northern portion of Scotland near the ocean.

Lizzie Skelton's father, Benjamin Franklin Skelton (1852-1929) lived a good ways into the 20th century. His last years were spent operating a grocery store in Tuscaloosa. He seems to have married twice, but Lizzie's mother was Mary Elizabeth Broughton (1859-1914), who died at fifty-five.

It's interesting that on Lizzie Skelton's side there is a grandmother with the last name of Coker. I don't know if knowledge of Huldah Elizabeth Coker (born 1826), wife of James Riley Skelton (1827-1914), might have suggested my grandfather's eventual name or not.

Whenever I think of my maternal grandfather's side of the family, I think of that company town Brownville, near Tuscaloosa, although that was only a blip on the family's long history in America. It was where my line of Montgomerys weathered the Great Depression, however. And, of course, I think of Randolph County, Alabama, when I think of the Daniels. When I think of Mama Cooley's side of the family I picture the mountainous region of Gadsden, Alabama, and the Sand Mountain landscape north of there. It's the very end of the Appalachians. Anniston, Alabama, my hometown, is part of that final evolution of foothills, as well.

The Montgomerys came down from the Charlotte, North Carolina, area and, after a decade-long stop along the way, settled in the sandy, swampy soil of the Sipsey Swamp and environs near Tuscaloosa, while the Daniels and Barrons were farmers of the rocky red clay of northeastern Alabama. None of my ancestors came from the far south of the state. The closest thing we have to a planter in the family is Barnabas Barron, who was a well-to-do farmer in Georgia. But then the Civil War hit him, and his family was scattered to the winds.

⚛ Part 3 ⚛
Martha and Jerry Daniel

Martha Ann Montgomery (born 1941)
and Jerry Anthony Daniel (1940-2019)

To fully characterize my parents would require an entire book
in itself. I would get lost in doing it, perhaps for years. What
I want to do here is provide a sketch. Some things must be lost
in time, maybe, or you reach the point where nothing can be
saved, because saving everything becomes such a gargantuan
task you never do it. Yet there are so many gems I recall that,
when I provide an overview, it does not seem to me that the
qualities, observations, and moments I mention are more
important than the ones that I leave out. So much is
important. One has to do the best one can, I suppose.

Martha

⊰⊱⟡⟡⊰⊱

Martha Ann Montgomery (born 1941)

Martha Ann Montgomery Daniel was the first child of Coker Montgomery and Louise Cooley Montgomery. Little Martha Montgomery was a precocious child. You can look at her youthful photographs and tell that. You can see it in her smile—Martha's intelligence and sense of humor.

Martha grew up in Birmingham, Alabama. The Montgomerys and Electa Cooley lived together in one small house or another in North Birmingham. My mother doesn't remember any particular house that she has told me about. She calls the neighborhood ACIPCO when she talks about it. She did quite well in school from a young age, and Louise was proud of her, of course.

She was a city girl. With the brief exception of Coker's foray back into farming, she was the daughter of an electrician in the coal mines, and then an electrician in the steel mills. She lived among that industrial superstructure that formed Birmingham, Alabama. For the most part, this meant living in the ACIPCO area of Birmingham, also called North Birmingham.

In her very young years, during World War II, my aunt and Coker's half-sister, Maria Montgomery Bottoms, lived with them for a couple of years. My mother spent the rest of her life feeling in awe of Maria as a result. When my mother had respect for someone or some institution, it would awaken an anxiety in her that left her almost unable to interact with them, at times.

I remember when we went on a vacation to California and were passing through Los Angeles, she was in state of apprehension as to whether or not to call Maria and Gene, and stop by. She felt inadequate to Maria's intellect and refinement, I think. The Bottomses visited us occasionally, if the families could intersect on one of their trips to Alabama. I remember playing with Mike and worshipping Frances when they came to visit us at the campground at Gulf Shores State Park. Frances, Frankie they called her then, was eighteen or so at the time, and she was transcendently beautiful. I could barely look at her without feeling overwhelmed. Mike and I got along great. He was a little bit older than me, and he was very much the guy who would lead you in exciting, fun stuff. I later got to know them both as adults, of course. I even put Gene, Mike, and Frances's son, Jason Meunier, in films I did while I was at USC Film School.

After the war, Janice Fay Montgomery (1947-2015) came along, and Martha had a sister. Martha continued going to North Birmingham schools until high school. At that point, she attended the big collector high school in downtown Birmingham. This was Phillips High School. Of course, when she started, the school was segregated. Black children went to other schools in the South until desegregation. The policy was called "separate but equal." This was a joke. There was nothing equal about it. I have seen many of those black schools from the period that have either been converted or closed down. They were second-class in their architecture and accoutrements. They got the tattered books left over from the white schools, for instance. It was a shameful policy, and we are well rid of this horrible practice in the South.

On the other hand, segregation should not be exaggerated, or the historic point will lose its impact. Segregation in the American South was far from throwing people into internment camps and executing them, or some of the other practices of totalitarian states. If it is equated with such, and pronounced an unthinkable horror, one will not think about it, and something like it involving other races, other groups, may come back in other forms, because the so-called unthinkable goes down the memory hole of society, goodbye. We can draw nothing useful from the past when rational assessment is overwhelmed by emotion.

My mother rode a city bus, not a school bus, from her home in North Birmingham to a stop in front of the Catholic church in downtown Birmingham. She was often early due to the bus schedule, and she would go inside the sanctuary for shelter. Sometimes she would pray there, or meditate. She has done this in other Catholic churches throughout her life.

The nuns at the church in Birmingham were always kind to her, she says. This developed in her an affinity for Catholicism. She later became Catholic for a while, among other denominations she tried out (with my family tagging along) over the years.

My mother was at Phillips when it was integrated in 1959. She remembers it well, when the first black children came. She had no problem with it.

You have to imagine what life in Birmingham was like at that time. People in the South of different races grew up with each other. They were not physically separated, but interacted all the time. They were entirely used to being around one another. Segregation did not mean white people did not see black people everywhere, or that black people did not encounter white people in all manner of places. Most of the time, everyone got along just fine. Segregation was an ugly policy imposed over general human amity. I saw this in action growing up in the South a decade after segregation. Anyway, I don't know why my mother never developed a trace of racial bigotry, given that my grandparents were certainly typical prejudiced people of their time, but she didn't.

In high school, my mother was involved in all sorts of clubs. I've seen some of her yearbooks and have been surprised at the great many activities she was part of. She must have thought at one point she might want to be a teacher because she was involved with the future teachers club, for instance. I asked her about her activities once, and she said she did anything that looked interesting to her. She was a very engaged student, and she made quite good grades. I'm sure she was considering going to college even then. She had the example of Maria Montgomery, who graduated from the University of Alabama.

She was clearly a very talented young woman, and I think everyone had high hopes for her. She herself nursed a secret ambition to be a lawyer later in life (after she gave up on social work), and she tried to push me in that direction, as well. Perhaps I should've listened.

When she finally got her degree from Jacksonville State, it was with a major in political science. It was at that point, I believe, that she was considering going to law school. She never did. It would have been difficult. David and I had to go to college with her help. And both of us were in a private school, Donoho, at the time, where we had to pay partial tuition.

For many years, her ambition had been to be a social worker. But after her run-ins with actual social workers while she and my father tried to adopt a little girl during the 1970s, she ended up loathing the profession.

For some reason, the regional social worker in Anniston took a dislike to my family and would not let my parents adopt. My mother and father had an orphan girl from Mexico picked out, and were determined to bring her into the family. They filled out all the paperwork. We made family pictures in front of our house. We provided all the financial documentation you could want. But the local social worker had final say. She arbitrarily decided against allowing us to adopt the little Mexican girl.

This nearly broke my mother's heart at the time. It is one of the reasons that I am so set against government interference in people's lives. Government does far more harm than good, if it does any good at all on a social level. It needs to be kept away from any meaningful decision about human families. How could that woman have known anything about us? She knew nothing. She told my mother she had a feeling that something wasn't right with us. And she denied permission for the adoption.

Good Lord. What a horrible person she was.

I won't dignify her by writing her name here, but I remember it well enough. I later had to go to high school with her daughter, who was an idiot. And then I went to college and was friends with a guy whose mother was the social worker's roommate in college. For a while there, it seemed I could not get away from this horrid woman's influence who had denied my mother's happiness. But now I have hardly thought about her in many decades. I do hope she's dead, and that maybe it was something painful that took her away.

The reason that my mother wanted to adopt was that, after having David, she was told that she should not have any other children, that it was dangerous if a developing child had the opposite blood type from her, and that she and the baby might die as a result. I don't know the truth of this, but it put off my parents from having any more children. My mother took birth control pills her entire adult life, so they could regulate when they wanted to have children, and they had no more after my brother.

We did, however, keep several foster children while I was growing up, particularly when I was younger. In Tuscaloosa, we had a little girl named Donna who lived with us for over a year. David and I came to think of her as our sister. And I think she truly felt like one of us, as well. I remember when the social worker came to take her away. Donna was clutching this big bear that she'd gotten at the county fair we'd all attended together. I'd gotten a yellow one, and David had a blue one, and she had gotten a big pink one. She was only three then. She was crying, trying to be brave. I will never forget that moment. I wish she could've stayed, and remained one of us. This was at our Alpine Hills house. I must've been six or seven years old at the time.

After we moved to Anniston, we took in a series of foster girls also, some of them from a local orphanage run by a kindly preacher. They were not truly orphans, but just children whose parents had abandoned them for one reason or another. One in particular I remember, whose name was Nina, had a mother who pushed her arm through a wringing machine, an apparatus for squeezing water from clothes before you hung them to dry. Horrific things those children went through.

My mother longed to have a daughter, and she continued to bring girls home until we left Anniston, but never took it up again when she moved to Texas. By that time, she had discovered dogs as a surrogate. This proved to be quite unfortunate.

As mentioned, my mother was involved with several clubs at Phillips High School. Like many bright teenagers, I think she joined whatever struck her fancy and tried to be active. Probably a lot of it was just staying away from home and my drunken grandfather. I don't know. Her sister Janice did not go to Phillips. The family had moved by then, and I believe Janice went to Woodlawn High School on the east side of Birmingham.

One of the high school organizations my mother joined was the youth contingent of the Civil Air Patrol. This was rather a big deal in the 1950s. I'm not exactly sure why. It may have had something to do with Cold War sensibilities, but more likely it reflected the lack of technology that led many more airplanes than nowadays to crash and disappear.

The Civil Air Patrol would go out and do aerial search and rescues for downed planes and pilots. It was an organization that had uniforms, and was a lot like the Boy Scouts, or military, although it included girls, obviously. My mother must have gone to the same nine-day encampment that my dad went to (I have a news story documenting his attendance), because that's how they met, via the CAP. They met in Montgomery, Alabama, at Maxwell Air Force Base, at a mixer for the youth who came to the Civil Air Patrol encampment in mid-August 1958. After that, my dad began going to Birmingham, staying with my Aunt Ethel, I believe, and courting my mother, perhaps on the sly from his parents.

I'm very sure there was no sex involved before they got married, but it was probably fairly hot and heavy otherwise, seeing as they were both teenagers. I believe that it was in the second part of 1958 that Jerry seriously began courting Martha, coming from Auburn where he had gone for a first year of college.

It may even be that his obsession with seeing my mother was causing his grades to suffer, I don't know. He told me once that he was not happy at all at Auburn, and he dropped out after that first year. This caused my grandparents to stop paying for his tuition. They had been pressuring him to do what they wanted, and by this point he was done with that. I would've been too.

So after a year at Auburn, and after my mother graduated from high school, the two of them decided to elope to Georgia. My mother always said no one was opposed to their being together, but that they had decided to elope because they thought it would be romantic. My mother afterwards regretted not having a church wedding of some sort, but that's what they decided to do in July of 1959. They got in a car, perhaps my father's, and drove to Trenton, Georgia. As I recall the story, they got there fairly late at night and had to wake up a preacher who was a justice of the peace. Probably my father had heard about him somewhere. He got up, and then he woke up his wife, who was in curlers. She served as the witness in the marriage ceremony.

And Martha and Jerry drove back and moved in together. I'm not sure where they lived at first. My father dropped out of Auburn, and he and my mother moved to Tampa, Florida.

They lived there for about two years. My mother got a job at the Indian River Fruit Exchange and my father worked using his drafting skills. They ultimately wanted more education, and so they headed back north, finally to Tuscaloosa, where they both enrolled in the University of Alabama. My mother worked in the athletic department as a secretary, and my father got a job at the Alabama Geological Survey as a draftsman. They moved into a small trailer at the Married Student Trailer Park at the University of Alabama. The address was 13 Trailer Park Court, I think.

It was sometime in early 1963 that my mother became pregnant with me. She'd waited almost four years after getting married. I was born at Druid City Hospital in Tuscaloosa on November 25, 1963.

Taking care of me and working the job was too much for my mother to do and still be able to stay in school, so she dropped out. She went back sporadically after that, but it was not until I was in high school that she was able to finish her bachelor's degree at Jacksonville State University, a medium-sized state school north of Anniston, Alabama. While she was at Alabama, she began study to become a social worker.

Martha and Jerry were in Tuscaloosa, a college town, during the tumultuous 1960s. They were witness to college protests. I believe my mother attended a later-period civil rights march, but found some of the participants shouting obscenities and hateful remarks, and so she decided to leave. My mother worked in part for Paul Bear Bryant, the famous football coach. It was during the time that she was working as a secretary in the athletic department that Joe Namath, the legendary quarterback, was at Alabama. She remembers she saw him all the time there, and she recalls once he needed to go across the hall from one locker room to another, and he was only partially dressed—particularly not dressed on the bottom portion. He thought he would be able to dart across the corridor, but then he saw my mother there. Broadway Joe blushed, and went to grab something to cover himself. He came back and apologized. My mother said not to worry about it, and Namath gave her a big smile.

When my parents got back to Alabama from Florida, they apparently decided they needed to go back to church. Neither of them liked the emotive excess of the Baptist churches they'd been raised in, however. So my mother picked out the Episcopal Church to join. They'd done this before when they briefly lived in Anniston, and decided to go to St. Michael's and All Angels there. I was baptized at

St. Michael's when I was an infant. This was one of two baptisms I've experienced. The first was Episcopalian and the second Baptist. Surely the double dunk will seal my entry into the Kingdom.

In Tuscaloosa, we attended St. Matthias Episcopal Church. I remember it well. I remember Reverend Lilly, the priest there. He wore round, steel-rimmed glasses. I recall my mother dressing up in the proper Episcopalian fashion of the time, which meant that the woman wore a hat to church with a small lacy veil on it shrouding the eyes. She also wore gloves to church, white ones. It was a cute and smart look. I hope it will return some day.

After my father graduated, he got another job, this time at the U.S. Geological Survey, with offices in, I believe, W.B. Jones Hall on the University of Alabama campus. We were considered in the faculty and staff category, and I learned to swim at the University of Alabama faculty swimming pool. Eventually, Jerry became head of the drafting department at the Geological Survey, and he also worked part time for the state geologist of Alabama, Phillip LaMoreaux.

Martha had several jobs after the University of Alabama. She worked in the Woolco Department Store at McFarland Mall for quite a while as a cashier. My great-grandmother came over to take care of us, but we also had a series of black maids who my parents were able to hire for not very much in wages. I really don't know how my parents afforded it, but they did. There was one maid in particular whom I adored. Her name was Lulu. She played games like Candyland with me, and we had a wonderful time together while she was keeping me.

My parents briefly moved to St. Louis, Missouri. This was just after my father graduated. He found a drafting job there, working for a steel engineering firm. They did not like St. Louis, and my father really disliked his coworkers there. He said they were smart alecks, and generally unpleasant to be around. They probably insulted him because he was from the South, because he called them "all a bunch of smartass Yankees I didn't want to be around" later when I asked him about it. They lived in an apartment near the Budweiser plant. Once, when I was in graduate school in St. Louis and my mother was visiting, we drove to the neighborhood and found the place.

Martha and Jerry then moved to Anniston, and I think he briefly went to work at Daniel Electric again. That didn't last long. My father then moved to Birmingham, and worked for a while at the Chicago

Iron and Bridge Company, as a draftsman in their Birmingham office. This may have been another place my father quit because he didn't like the atmosphere. There were times when my mother recalled this place and the job in St. Louis, and darkly referred to my father's lack of ambition. But I really don't know the circumstances. I suspect my father had many issues with authority and bosses after dealing with Emmett and Myrtice during his teens, and probably rebelled against authoritarian types at work.

But Tuscaloosa called. Literally. Here's my father's version.

It's interesting to me that both Tony and David were born in Tuscaloosa. It wasn't planned that way. It's just that Tony was born when I was in school at the University of Alabama, and then we went to St. Louis, and we went to Anniston, and then we moved to Birmingham. Then the place where I worked when I was a student at the University of Alabama, the fellow there, called me and said the old man that was in charge of the art department was retiring and would I come back and take his place.

So we moved to Tuscaloosa, and David was born while we were there. So both of them were—what's the difference between you and David? Four years?

Tony: Three and a half years.

Three and a half years. And we had lived all over the country, but both the children were born in Tuscaloosa. Maybe nobody else would care about that. They were born in Druid City Hospital. And they both were weaned from the bottle by throwing the bottle into the Black Warrior River at the bridge between Tuscaloosa and Northport. Your mother did that.

My mother told me, and later my brother, that the baby fish in the Black Warrior River needed my bottle, and made me feel like I was giving them a great gift. She also bought me a lunchbox that I had been craving that featured the children's entertainer Captain Kangaroo, his sidekick, Mr. Greenjeans, and his puppet friend, Mr. Moose. I used the Captain Kangaroo lunchbox and the thermos bottle inside for many years.

So Martha and Jerry moved back to Tuscaloosa, and Jerry returned to W.B. Jones Hall and went to work for the U.S. Geological Survey. I grew up in Tuscaloosa, Alabama, until I was ten years old.

Martha had me when she was twenty-two. I was not born in the small student trailer, of course, but in Druid City Hospital. I believe my parents had coverage of the expenses from my father's part-time job at the Geological Survey, or they paid for it from savings. They were not typical college students, but a little older.

In the trailer park, they had become friends with another couple, Mary Jim Kelly Tucker and Donnie Franklin Tucker. The Tuckers were both from South Alabama. When I was born, they became the godparents at my baptism in the Episcopal church. They also became David's godparents. Donnie and Mary Jim settled in Birmingham, and we visited them fairly often until my parents moved to Texas. They had two daughters that almost matched the ages of myself and David. These were Donna and Amy Tucker, and we consider them our god-sisters. Donna was blonde, and Amy was darker complexioned, and freckled. Donnie owned an excavation contracting company, and Mary Jim ran a fairly enormous dance school. We attended several of their recitals over the years. I believe Mary Jim and my mother were thick as thieves during their time in the trailer park, and remained friends for many years after. The Tucker family went through a lot of turmoil, which I won't go into here. I last saw a remarried Mary Jim at Electa Cooley's funeral.

Martha was mostly preoccupied with working and raising David and me during her twenties and early thirties. When I was old enough, she became a Den Mother in the Cub Scouts. I was in, I believe, Pack 30, Den 4, in Tuscaloosa. My father was the Cubmaster of the pack, as he would later become the Scoutmaster of my Boy Scout troop in Anniston.

Martha also was involved at my schools, and became president of the PTA for one year at one of them, Skyland Elementary, I believe. During this time, she held down various jobs. I think she worked at the McFarland Mall Woolco the longest.

After Jerry graduated, and they returned to Tuscaloosa, they moved into an apartment on Edgewood Avenue. I have no memory of the place. Then we moved to a starter house in a lower middle class neighborhood called Alpine Hills in East Tuscaloosa, 4323 31st Ave E, not far from Cottondale. That is where my memories begin.

My father once told me he had been talking to a banker, and was completely surprised to learn that, with his job, he could qualify for a mortgage. They found the house, which was a very basic affair built in what had once been a pine forest planted for pulpwood. The houses were arranged in a circle, and their backyards all opened onto a stand of trees that the builders had left standing. We called this the Pine Grove. I spent many hours in those trees. My father raked out bike paths in the heavy build-up of pine needles, and built us all kinds of playing places, such as a wonderful locomotive made from an old water heater, and an A-frame treehouse.

It was during this time that my parents founded a small business in the university district of downtown Tuscaloosa. They rented a retail space and started a slot car racing track. I think they called this the Tuscaloosa Speedway, or something like that. Slot cars were a craze at the time. These were miniature racing cars with electric motors inside them. They were about the size of most model cars at the time, ten inches long or so. There was a bladelike slide with a copper contact on it that extended down from the chassis in the front part of the car through which electricity was delivered that powered the car. This was fitted into a small slot on a race track.

My parents had purchased a slot car track. It was huge, especially to me at three or four years of age. It took up most of the space they had rented. Really, it was quite something. At night, aficionados of slot cars would come, bringing their cars, and pay to enter races. They controlled the flow of electricity by a pumper switch held in their hands, which was a rheostat of some sort. The challenge was to race around the track as fast as you could go without slinging your car out of its slot during the race. There was, I think, some finesse to it. And some of the racers rigged their cars for pure speed.

It's a subculture I don't pretend to grasp. I think it was a combination of oldtime pool hall culture and pre-video-game geekiness. I remember my father sitting on a big, manila-brown stool, holding up a turquoise HB drafting pencil to signal the participants that the race was about to start. Then he would lower his arm with the pencil in it, and the race would begin. He also held a clipboard on which he carefully noted the race results. There were no cash prizes—that would have been gambling—but there were small trophies and discounts on the merchandise my parents also sold. In fact, the merchandise was where they made what money there was to be had from this operation.

They ran the slot car track for perhaps two or three years. I believe that the man who owned the building abruptly raised the rent on them. My father was still paying off the slot car track and dealing with the other expenses. In the end, they foolishly declared bankruptcy (this harmed their finances for years after) and sadly closed down the Tuscaloosa Speedway forever.

Daddy stored the slot car track in the loft of the Daniel Electric warehouse for years until he finally got tired of paying his parents rent (yes, of course they charged him for it), and sold the tracks (there were two, one large, one smaller) for practically nothing to someone who wanted it for a game room in his basement. By that time, the slot car craze was long past.

One of my most vivid memories from my time as a toddler was when my father lifted me up and put me on the slot car track one day before the races were started. I ran around that track in my bare feet several times, leaving dusty footprints they then had to whisk off. Taking the big canted bank on the track was a lot of fun. If you kept running, you wouldn't fall.

I also remember the worshipful faces some of the young guys who came to race had for my father. He was the king of the world they wished to conquer. They were probably stealing glances at my mother, who worked behind the sales counter. She was quite the beauty then. It was a very male oriented place, although I think some of the racers brought their girlfriends along to cheer. There were audiences for the races, I recall.

When I think of Tuscaloosa, I think of sandy soil and pine trees. It seemed to me that the whole city was built on the bottomlands of the Black Warrior River. And the portion of the county where my grandfather grew up was tucked away in the Sipsey Swamp. The Tuscaloosa of my childhood is mainly a memory of Alpine Hills, Alberta City, the university campus where my father worked, and the university business district, which had restaurants and bars siding it, such as Broadway Joe's and Morrisons Cafeteria. My mother particularly like to take us to Morrisons because you got a lot for the buffet price.

I remember it being hot all the time. I was mostly barefoot. I could run over gravel, the soles of my feet were so tough. In Alberta City, the air was pervaded with the smell of the pulpwood processing from the nearby paper plant. Here pine trees were turned into cardboard, toilet paper, and all manner of things woody and papery. That smell you can never forget once you've sniffed it. Even thinking about it now can sometimes make me gag.

Tuscaloosa at that time revolved around both the university and the forestry industry. Vast tracts of the land about it were pine tree farms deliberately planted, left to grow for several years, then harvested—and the cycle was repeated again. It used to be highly agricultural, with plenty of cotton grown there. There's a town named Cottondale on the outskirts of Tuscaloosa, for instance. There's a Mercedes Automobile plant near there now.

But the main driver of everything in Tuscaloosa is the University of Alabama. My parents were intimately connected with it from the moment they came to the town to the moment they left.

The name Tuscaloosa itself means "Black Warrior," and it is the name of the Mississippian Indian tribe leader who confronted De Soto in South Alabama when the conquistador first traversed the South in the 1500s. Chief Tuscaloosa was said to be a giant of a man.

In 1971, we moved from the house in Alpine Hills to a bigger brick house in the Alberta City neighborhood of Tuscaloosa. This moved us to a new school district and threw me into East End Elementary, a place I soon detested, and my mother along with me. This move also took my mother away from the friendships she'd established in the east Tuscaloosa area. She had been very social there, and I think she suffered in the new location.

During my two years at Jolly Time Kindergarten, and then my one-and-a-half years at Skyland Elementary, my mother had become good friends with the mother of a playmate of mine, Cathy Deas. They found it hard to get together after the move, and I left my friend Tommy behind at my old school. Although I made friends in the new neighborhood, I think it was an unfortunate move for my parents. I had a couple of disastrous teachers—one of whom took an active, cruel dislike to me—and my mother was quite distressed that I was unhappy at school.

One very stark and clear memory I have from Alpine Hills was the night my mother, my brother, and I were home alone. My father was working late, I believe. The house had a carport covering and the door from the carport led into the kitchen. It was not solid, but was covered with a louvered window of slotted glass panes. You could turn a crank and open it up to let air in (there was a screen on the kitchen side to keep out the flies in summer). The glass panes, about a handbreadth wide, and a couple of feet long, were frosted. At night, if the light was on in the carport and someone came to the door, you could see their frosted outline through the glass.

One night, when my father was away working late, and my mother, David and I, were home alone, someone came to the door and began to knock at it. My mother gathered my brother and me behind her in the kitchen. We peeked around her to see the outline of a man. He was shaking the locked doorknob and calling out to be let in.

"You've got the wrong address," my mother loudly told him.

He laughed, and said she had to be kidding. This was the right house, the house he was looking for.

She later explained that the guy was drunk out of his mind, which she knew at the time, of course. I was just bewildered by it all. He banged again and again. Why wouldn't the man go away? There was the real possibility he would break through the glass window and be able to reach inside and open the door from within.

My mother was armed with a pistol for most of her life. At that time, she owned a coal-black .22 automatic. She took it from her purse and pointed it at the figure on the other side of the door.

"I've called the police. I have a gun here, and I will shoot you," she told the guy.

In fact, I think there were two men out there, but only one was banging at the door. This guy laughed. My mother pulled back the hammer.

"I'm going to shoot you if you don't go away *right now*," she told him.

After a grunt of disgust, the guy left. And thereby likely saved his own life. Possibly. My mother discovered later that she still had the safety set on the pistol. She soon got rid of the .22 and bought a .38 revolver, a far easier gun to use. That is what she packed for many decades in her purse.

I'm not sure where my mother was working while we were in Alberta City. She may have become a full-time housewife during that time to tend to David and me. Those were his toddler years. I don't remember Mama Cooley being there to housesit nearly as much in Alberta City. This was the 1970s, and the days of a lower middle class family being able to hire cheaply a responsible black woman for a babysitter and housekeeper were gone in the South.

Twice the U.S. Geological Survey sent my father on extended trips for training, and we accompanied him. I'm not sure of the chronology, but I think the first time was to Denver, Colorado. We lived out of a Motel Six there. My mother took us to museums and such while my father was at work, and once or twice we drove out to the ski slopes to watch people skiing. Once we went out at night to watch the night skiing. It was bitter cold, but I was fascinated by the skiers coming down under the big arc lights on the slope.

The other extended trip was to Washington, D.C. Again, we stayed in a hotel, a Days Inn. It would probably be a crime-ridden hellhole now, but the neighborhood was all right. We spent three weeks touring everything in Washington with my mother. She took us to every monument, to the Capitol Building, to the Smithsonian, to many other museums. We also played in many area playgrounds in the city parks. These had amazing tornado slides that we'd never seen in Alabama. And they had old jet airplanes. The guts had been taken out, and the jets were mounted on concrete piers. You could crawl all over them. Most fun of all—you could crawl *through* the jet air intakes and out the exhaust port on either wing, or vice versa. David and I loved threading through those jet engine cavities.

While we were there, Martha went to the Library of Congress and the National Archives, where she began doing genealogical research. She discovered a great deal there, and wrote down what she could. She discovered a thorough book on the Montgomerys that had listed Taylor and Fannie, Maria and Gene, but had missed Lizzie's children and grandchildren, Coker and Revis. My mother may have written to the author to tell him of his gap. She couldn't spend a lot of time there because she had David and me with her constantly.

Then there is the big story of Washington. On our tour of the White House, we were lined up and passing inside. There was no metal detector, or it was out of order, perhaps. In any case, everyone with bags or purses had to pass them by a security guard who poked around inside each one.

Well, just as she came up to the guy and presented her purse to be inspected, Martha realized she had brought her .38 revolver along in the purse. The guard opened the purse and began to poke around inside. Martha held her breath. What would happen if they discovered the gun? Could she talk her way out of this?

But she was a young woman with two young boys trailing along with her, clearly her own. Obviously no threat.

Yet, there was that revolver sitting in the purse.

Then there was a commotion behind her in line. Someone asked the guard a question, quite loud. The guy hesitated a moment, then closed Martha's purse and passed it back to her. He motioned for us to go on in while he dealt with whatever was going on behind us in line.

And that is how my mother came to carry a .38 revolver with her throughout a tour of the Nixon White House in May of 1972.

It was while we were in Washington that Alabama Governor George Wallace was shot while campaigning for president in Maryland. My mother disliked Wallace greatly, and had voted against him in every election, but she debated whether or not she, as a loyal Alabamian, should visit him in the hospital. In the end, she decided she should. She called, but found they weren't taking visitors. In fact, Wallace had been gravely injured, paralyzed for life below the waist, and would spend years recovering a semblance of health. He was in no shape to see her at the time.

One thing I remember equally well from that trip is the smell of tear gas. There were riots going on while we were there. Once, when we were at the top of the Washington Monument, there was a bomb threat. There was an elevator up, but we had decided to climb down the whole way on the stairs beforehand. An FBI agent was at the bottom doorway, unaware there were clueless stragglers still coming down. He urged us to jog quickly away as we emerged.

This was also the first time I encountered how dirty Northern cities could be. There were bums living on the Capitol Mall, and several times we came across human feces lying on the steps and marble walls of monuments.

Throughout the trip, Martha maintain her aplomb and determination that her boys experience her nation's capital to the greatest extent possible. We also encountered cartoon series on television in the hotel room that I'd never seen before. That there could be different cartoons in different places was a revelation to me.

During some of this time, my parents drove a plum-color Mustang convertible. It was a cute little car, and would probably be worth many thousands of dollars if we had it today. We took that Mustang to Denver, I remember, but some other car, perhaps our station wagon, to Washington, D.C.

Once, when I was at home with Mama Cooley in Alpine Hills, my parents and David had gone somewhere together, maybe to the mall. On the way, a motorcycle pulled out in front of them. My father was driving and my mother was in the passenger seat. David was in the back, and so was our foster daughter, Donna.

My father ran into the motorcycle and threw both motorcycle and driver high into the air, about fifty feet, my father estimated later. The motorcycle came crashing down longways across the Mustang's windshield. It completely shattered the windshield, but the glass held, and the bike didn't continue through to crush my parents. The driver landed somewhere nearby, and badly broke his leg. I remember them arriving home, shaken and filled with adrenaline, no doubt. I became frightened just listening to them tell about what had happened, and Mama Cooley kept saying, "Lord! Oh, Lordy!" as each scary detail unfolded.

My mother was particularly solicitous of Donna, who had seen enough trauma in her life with her horrible parents. Donna seemed to be stunned, as she often did when overwhelmed with emotions. She was a tiny girl, all of three or four, who cringed easily at any perceived threat. I had caused her to on several occasions, until I felt guilty and learned better. David was still crying a little, but mostly unaffected.

We encountered the motorcycle driver several weeks later walking around on crutches in a store. My mother asked after him, and he said he was starting to feel better, but the leg still hurt. My mother expressed sympathy.

"Don't worry. It was all my fault, ma'am," I remember him bashfully telling her. He said he was looking to get another motorcycle, however, when he could ride again.

This is one reason that I have never particularly wanted a motorcycle. Even a little drop-top Mustang can beat them in a crash.

Once we moved to Anniston, I was in a far better school, and we were in a nicer neighborhood. Martha began to make friends again.

She became particular friends with Jo Faye Walker, the mother of one of my playmates, and a couple of other women. In Anniston, she studied real estate and obtained her license. She went to work for a local broker, Gary Pugh. For several years she sold houses for Pugh Real Estate. Near the Gary Pugh offices was Anniston's lone Catholic church. There, my mother resumed her practice of going inside, kneeling at a pew bench, and saying a prayer daily. She was very regular about it.

We transferred to Grace Episcopal Church and then to St. Michael's Episcopal, before my mother gave up on Episcopalianism once and for all. Episcopalians in Anniston were a much different bunch than the liberal, open college Episcopalians of St. Mattias, our church for the entire time we lived in Tuscaloosa. Anniston Episcopalians were snobs. There's no other way to put it. Class conscious snobs of the worst kind. To top it all, my mother was in a Sunday school class one day when the teacher confessed that he really didn't believe in God.

"Then why are you *teaching* a Sunday School class?" she asked him, and he shrugged. He was teaching because the rich families in town had to belong to the Episcopal Church, of course, and it was expected. My mother realized this, and soon left that nest of hypocrites behind. Unfortunately, this mostly meant my father was done with church. He could not abide evangelicals, although he did occasionally come to Golden Spring Baptist after I got heavily involved in the youth group there as a teenager. It was also the sponsoring institution of Troop 9, where he was Scoutmaster, and he felt he ought to be a member, I think. But he never liked Baptists.

We did not immediately become Baptists, however. We tried the Presbyterians for a while. Then we went to a Catholic church in Jacksonville, which had the college church feel that they'd enjoyed at St. Mattias. But ultimately, the large youth group and plentiful activities for David and me drew us to Golden Springs Baptist.

I had a salvation experience there at the age of eleven, and was baptized again in the sanctuary tank, full-immersion this time, when I was twelve or so. That church was very important to my personal development. I became quite the young intellectual evangelical there. But I don't think it was as meaningful to my mom. Ritual and calm appealed to her, drawing her back to that sense of peace she felt at the Catholic sanctuary near Phillips High as a girl. But she continued attending Golden Springs Baptist because David and I were enjoying the youth activities so much.

We went on several family vacations to the western United States throughout the 1970s. The first one, which I've mentioned before, was in 1968. The whole Daniel clan went in caravan fashion Out West together. That turned out to be not very great for the adults, but Martha and Jerry found that they really loved the American West. They decided to go back.

There were three main trips that the family took. The first one was while we lived in Tuscaloosa. The second two were after we moved to Anniston. The biggest one was when we spent July of 1974 traveling.

I recall in Tuscaloosa when my father came home one day with a small silver pop-up trailer camper attached to the hitch of his car. This was not one of those self-popping campers that you see today, but something you had to fold out manually and set up. It expanded into two sleeping pallets, with foam mattresses that were a little short of full size. Over this, you erected a canvas, tent-like structure that made it all into a cabin-like space, but on wheels. It slept four, rather tightly. My father and mother had been camping many times before. They had a canvas cabin tent they used to go to the Smokies. They made this trip several times before and after I was born.

In fact, one morning while camping at the Smokies, Martha was inside that cabin tent taking out her curlers and putting on makeup. She had a small makeup mirror on a little table, and, as she looked into it to apply something, she saw a bear looking back at her. It was in the entrance of the tent, poking its head in. She turned around and looked at the bear, and the bear looked at her. She told it to go away. After a moment, away it went. Evidently the bear had surmised that there was no food in the tent, which was probably what it was looking for. Those bears are raiders of camping food in the Smokies. I've seen them go after coolers and tear them to pieces to get what's inside. They generally won't bother people, since there is no percentage in that.

I remember a couple of those Smokies campouts with my parents, especially once climbing up a steep hill in the Smokies with my dad.

So they were already well acquainted with camping when they decided to make their epic Western quests. It helped that there was a newly developing chain of campgrounds at the time that my mother loved. These were the KOAs, the Kampground of America franchise.

We were inveterate KOA stayers. The great thing about the KOAs was that they had hot showers, which most National Park campgrounds did not. You could also count on a hot shower at a state park, so we usually stayed at either state park campgrounds or KOAs. But at the big national parks we stayed in the national park campgrounds to be near the attraction. For instance, when we went to the Grand Canyon we stayed in the Mather Campground, despite its lack of showers.

The first time we went on vacation, my father borrowed a white Ford van from Daniel Electric. He brought it back to Tuscaloosa from Anniston, and he and my mother proceeded to cover it with hippie flower stickers they got from who-knows-where (I think maybe a record shop in the mall). Jerry returned the van later to my grandfather with these stickers on it, and my grandfather nearly blew a gasket when he saw it. Anyway, we drove through the American West for three weeks in that white, pop-art-flower covered van. This would've been in the very early 1970s. We visited spots like the Painted Desert and the Petrified Forest in Arizona, and we went out to California and saw Sequoia trees there.

The biggest Out West trip we took was in 1977. This was after we'd moved to Anniston in 1973. We brought along Mama Cooley, Electa Barron Cooley, and she saw all of the Southwest for the first time. On that trip we did an extended stay at the Grand Canyon for several days. Also, I'm pretty sure that was the trip when we went to Yellowstone National Park. There are pictures of me and David by Old Faithful from that visit. My dad was absolutely entranced with the algae filled hot pools there. He made many slides of them. My mother kept David and me marshaled and fed, ready to see things. What she liked most was seeing the Indians selling their wares on the square in Santa Fe, New Mexico, and at Four Corners, the spot where the New Mexico, Utah, Colorado, and Arizona borders meet. Martha always liked silver and turquoise jewelry, and she bought several items there that she wore for many years afterward.

It was a great childhood, going on these vacations with my parents. It awakened in me a love for America, and particularly the landscape of the Southwest. My mother usually dressed in a cute, casual outfit of some sort, often a bandanna around her head. She was very much a creature of fashion in her younger years. She continued to dress fashionably until she moved to Dallas, where she adopted a business sort of dress for work, and turned to sweatpants and such outside of work. In a lot of ways, after the 1970s, she stopped caring what society thought of her. I think this had to do with her disillusionment with my father at that time, as well.

But back then she was nattily dressed in cute little vacation outfits at all times. She kept me and my brother snappily dressed as well, often in contrasting, but similar, shirts and pants. She had a good eye for clothing.

Martha's hair had begun to darken by her thirties, but she had been blonde so far in life, so she decided to stay blonde for the rest of it. She began to dye her hair, and I only saw it in its natural color once or twice ever, and only briefly. Even now, in her old age, she prefers to be blonde.

On that trip with my great-grandmother out West, I think we went all the way to Los Angeles, and up to Yosemite. That was the first time Martha had ever seen the Pacific Ocean. She didn't know that it wasn't the same temperature as the Atlantic or the Gulf of Mexico. It is not warm, but quite cold. She took David and me down to the beach, and we ran in—and immediately jumped back out, screaming. The water was freezing cold. But, as she always did at the Gulf Coast, she found a spot between the dunes and sunbathed for a while.

We made many trips to Florida and to Alabama's Gulf Coast. We went to Gulf State Park a great deal, sometimes for a weekend, sometimes longer. Our one family trip to Disney World was a camping trip. We used the camper, and stayed in the Fort Wilderness campground there. One summer, we rented a beach cabin and lodged for an entire month in the town of Gulf Shores itself.

Another time we drove all the way down the coast of Florida to John Pennycamp State Park on the Keys. It's amazing how the trips add up from those years. I grew to deeply love traveling because of them.

Martha cherished the beach above all places. She liked to lay in the sun and get tanned. She loved to go into the water and have a swim every now and then. She was a good swimmer. She enjoyed watching David and me frolic by the waves, of course.

One place that my parents discovered, and returned to repeatedly for long weekend trips, was Port St. Joe, and the Port St. Joseph Peninsula State Park, in northwestern Florida. It was a little-known beach at the time, and frequently we had the entire beautiful, white expanse to ourselves. We went sailing in the little harbor the peninsula forms there, and generally had a wonderful time. We truly worked that little camper for all it was worth during the 1970s.

During these trips, Martha and Jerry functioned as a team. There was a green Coleman stove that my father lit, and my mother cooked on. It required a lot of pumping and adjusting, which my mother left to my dad. She cooked all manner of things on the stove. I remember the smell of Coleman fuel fumes very well.

Later, after she moved to Dallas, Martha gave up camping for the most part. My father still went on trips with the Boy Scouts, but she never went much of anywhere after that just to be traveling. When she did go, she went to the beach, and she would stay in hotels or make it a day trip. It was kind of sad for me, as an adult, to see how they dropped going places together. It had been such an iconic part of my childhood.

Probably the reason that she quit going camping was because David and I were no longer along. Yet I continued traveling places with my father. I climbed many mountains with him in the 1980s and 1990s, which I will detail later. The only time my mother ever went camping Out West again was a trip we took in 1998. This was the summer after I had met my wife, Rika. In fact, Rika and I were already married, but we planned to have a real wedding ceremony in the future for the sake of our parents, and they did not know we were hitched at the time.

We went to Arches National Park with my mother and father, and then up into Colorado. That was Martha's last time in the American West. On that trip, we also passed through the Painted Desert, which was her absolute favorite landscape out there. We did not make it to the Grand Canyon that time, however, which she also adored.

Martha has green eyes. She is about five foot six. Although she was completely blonde when she was younger, she is not fair-skinned. She inherited from Coker Montgomery the capacity to quickly take on a deep tan. I seldom saw her sunburn. She eagerly waited for warm weather, and remained tanned most of the year in her younger days. I remember her as being fairly darkly tanned throughout the 1970s. This didn't bring on any premature aging. It is only after her health troubles in later years that she began to look older. She has a birthmark on her left thigh, a small patch, quite dark, that I believe she shares with

David, so it may be hereditary. She's not otherwise freckled. It is remarkable how different in complexion she and her sister were, yet clearly both were from the same parents.

She was slightly nearsighted, but would never wear glasses. The problem wasn't bad enough to affect her driving tests. My father and brother have perfect eyesight, but mine is badly out of whack—a defect perhaps inherited from her side of the family.

When I was twelve, my parents had a falling out over some stupid behavior of my father's that came to light. I won't go into the details. My mother had done nothing but support my dad for years, and felt quite betrayed. It took him years to mend the rift he opened.

Martha had been deeply devoted to Jerry since their marriage, following along with him on his wish to travel, on the doomed slot car track, and elsewhere. She realized that the real problem they faced at the time was that she had allowed him to return to Anniston and fall back under the influence of his parents, who had taken up where they'd left off, berating and belittling Jerry, while depending on him to do most of their work, and to calm all the feathers they ruffled in the business world. Jerry was deeply unhappy working for his parents.

It took her five more years, but she finally got him to apply for a new job—far away. With her urging, he sent out samples of his work from his days at the Geological Survey. It was excellent material, of course. Jerry was a dedicated craftsman when it came to maps and drawing, and a true artist at heart. Plus, he had tons of experience from the Geological Survey.

During my senior year in high school, he was asked out to Dallas, Texas, for an interview at Hunt Oil Company as a cartographer for the international development division. He was immediately offered the job, and my parents moved to Dallas in 1982, leaving me behind for half a year to live with a friend to finish high school. They had no choice. My father was needed at Hunt immediately. He would spend twenty-two more mostly content years working there. Once again, Martha had given Jerry a far happier life than he would have had otherwise.

Dallas was a revelation to my parents. There was probably nothing like it anywhere else in the world in the 1980s. It was a boom town like no other. And they arrived at the height of the boom. My father worked in the oil industry, the creator of the boom, although Dallas was a financial center that dealt with the oil money, not the headquarters for many oil companies other than Hunt and Mobile.

They first moved to Richardson, a northern suburb. The town of Plano, to the north of Richardson, barely existed at the time, and was the edge of everything. It was amazing; Dallas just *ended*, and became dirt country roads and prairie out there.

My mother had no trouble finding a job in banking, which she eventually parlayed into a job in mortgage financing. My dad remained at Hunt, content to make maps. I know how short ten years can feel after you are older. A blink. His hiatus in Anniston maybe felt like a brief purgatory for him, although it was in that place and time that I was a teenager, so it acquired deeper importance in my own psyche. From the beginning to the end, my father's career was really about drawing, draftsmanship, and maps. He was only an electrical contractor by accident for a while.

In Dallas, Martha and Jerry had more money than they ever had before. They ate out, and began to go places they wouldn't dream of in Alabama. I don't know that we ate out at fancy restaurants more than five or six times during my entire childhood. Although they managed to complicate their life needlessly in Texas, they were, overall, far happier than they ever had been in Anniston. I believe perhaps they were happiest in Tuscaloosa when they were starting out, but Dallas was a close second. My mother was far less content than my father, though, because she was separated from her mother and grandmother, which was an intense connection that she never broke away from until her grandmother died.

Dallas is flat. The taxes are low, and they know how to build roads. The roads are wide. The trees are squat. The sky is wide.

There is a dividing line that stretches up from the Gulf of Mexico that goes almost directly between Dallas and Fort Worth. This is a line of humidity. Everything to the west is arid. Things to the east become more and more humid. Many in Dallas think that Dallas is humid. People from Alabama know they are crazy to think this.

Dallas is a land where it is impossible to predict the weather. There is no landscape to shape it. All is southern prairie. Great cells of weather form in the atmosphere over those prairie lands, and just blunder about with no geography to channel them. You wake up to a sunny day, and then suddenly you've got class five tornadoes homing in on you. The summers can be insanely hot. When I lived there one summer day got up to 114° F in the shade. The winters are entirely unpredictable. You can be wearing shorts on New Year, and then a snowstorm can come through and you will be making snowmen the next day.

Most of Dallas, when my parents moved there, was landscaped with squat ornamental pear trees. They were ubiquitous and, to me, ugly. They also are short-lived, and when I moved to Dallas in the 2000s, they were all starting to die of old age. They are slowly being replaced with better trees now, many of which are native to, or at least compatible with, the landscape.

In the 1980s, the whole place smelled of money. It smelled of energy and upbeat attitudes, frenetically upbeat, and lots and lots of money.

Dallas proved to be a great jumping off point for Out West trips. In Alabama, you had to travel for a day, or day and a half, to get to the point where you were actually at the edge of the West. From Dallas, you could get to Colorado in a long day of driving. My family and I employed this proximity many times. I think I could drive the stretch between Dallas and Amarillo and Taos in my sleep. I know I could drive the stretch between Birmingham and Dallas with only occasionally glancing up, because I did it more than once in college. I would *read a book* when driving from Birmingham to Dallas back then, and another on the way back.

The move to Dallas was not good for my brother, however, and marked the beginning of a great many troubles for David. My mother always felt guilty for taking him away from Donoho Middle School, where he was fairly popular and content, and plunking him down in Richardson High School, where he felt lost, and eventually fell in with a partying sort of crowd. Eventually she transferred him to a private Catholic high school, Bishop Lynch, where he graduated. But the damage was already done, she feared. And it was, in a sense. David, unmoored from the life he'd known in Anniston, was always a bit unsettled and alienated in Dallas. He experienced a romantic setback while at the University of Dallas that set him to struggling for years, and sent him bouncing from college to work and back to college for a time. My mother fretted with him every step of the way.

Meanwhile, I was cutting the apron strings pretty quickly, although

I made it back to Dallas with regularity. Then came the death of Coker, followed by Electa's decline. As already detailed, Martha moved back to Birmingham for close to three years to take care of her grandmother until she passed away. Martha and Jerry met once a month or so, both making the long drive to Vicksburg, Mississippi, or some other meet-up spot, to stay in a hotel and spend the weekend together. This was about the time Jerry began working in earnest on his pottery, and then his steel sculpture, developing both to a high degree, and eventually showing his sculpture in some Dallas area galleries, selling some pieces, and undertaking a real commission or two.

Martha never made many friends in Dallas, and none that were as close as those she'd made in her younger days in Alabama. She felt disconnected from her roots there for a long time, but, as her grandmother passed away and Louise began to decline, she was less affected by this feeling. Eventually, she and Jerry retired to an eleven-acre plot of land in East Texas, about halfway between Dallas and Houston.

There she began her own decline of a sort. She had long felt a mission to help abandoned dogs in the Dallas area. This mission became an obsession, and she and Jerry moved to the country with about twenty stray dogs. Jerry built an enormous kennel-filled barn to house them, about ten miles outside of Centerville, Texas, and the two spent the next decade taking care of this brood of misplaced, misfit mutts, most of whom were horrid dogs that were unadoptable.

The barn was quite nice at first. Unlike his father Emmett, my father built structures soundly, to local code, and to last. He also started work on a studio nearby to make his sculptures. It was built partially from deadfall oak he'd acquired from the land there and had made into beautiful boards at a local sawmill.

My parents were relentless workers, but taking care of so many dogs became an overwhelming task for the two of them. The activity eventually subsumed all their other retirement plans, and then, at about the age of sixty-five, Jerry's Alzheimer's Disease, always lurking in the genes he'd received from Emmett, and from George Francis before him, emerged.

Martha was a capable woman, but had never been good at mechanical matters, or household repairs, usually depending on Jerry. He was soon unable to fix anything, and the barn, with its tiny retirement apartment in which they lived, became dilapidated—something neither would have permitted in earlier times. I believe my mother spent a great deal of 2014 fighting a general infection from her edema sores. This produced delusional thoughts, and the inability to keep on many tasks. It also fed into her desire to "save" even more dogs. There were dogs in every space in the barn, including my parents' living area. Despite all this, the dogs were fed and their wastes more-or-less tended to, and the barn wasn't a total disaster until late 2014.

After an incident with the local sheriff, I went and got them. I brought Martha and Jerry back with me to North Carolina and shut the dog barn down. This meant that I had to put down about thirty dogs, and scatter fifty feral cats. It was a thoroughly gruesome task. I've written about it elsewhere. It still bothers me to think of it.

I later discovered Martha was burning up with fever when I returned with her on December 21, 2014. My wife, Rika, and I put her immediately into the hospital where, a week later, she suffered a heart attack. She was in the ICU for several weeks, barely hanging on to life. Rika arranged for calming music and a chaplain's visit in the ICU. Finally, the doctors attempted to remove her breathing tube for a last try at self-sustained breathing. We expected her to die. But, lo and behold, she started breathing on her own. She slowly regained consciousness, worked through a period of paranoid confusion, and returned, pretty much, to normal. It was amazing, nigh on miraculous. We believe that the high fever, heart attack, and bladder failure she experienced were brought on by infected sores caused by the edema of her extremely swollen legs, a condition inherited from Louise and Electa, who also suffered from it. Our heritage sometimes follows us around in the most literal ways.

During Martha's recovery, her sister, Janice Montgomery England (1947-2015), came to live with us for a time as a caregiver for Martha and Jerry. But within a few months, the geriatric doctor we'd found for Martha and Jerry also examined Janice. He discovered that she had advanced cancer, possibly brought about by Janice's years of heavy smoking. Janice decided to move back to Birmingham to end her days. Her cousin Betty—Electa's sister Mae's daughter—took her in. She did not last long. Janice died May 7, 2015.

Janice was a hair stylist for most of her life. She was very good at it and at times owned her own shop. She had the misfortune to become involved with some real losers early on, and was often recovering from a bad relationship. She was a heavy smoker, and tried to pull back, but never really stopped. She had a lovely pale complexion, and freckles—the classic redhead look. She also was constantly moving, and had an extremely fast metabolism. She stayed very thin her whole life, and often had to eat extra to avoid becoming emaciated.

She only had my cousin Chris, and was a good mother to him. His father was nowhere to be found, of course. Later on, she remarried Andy Boggs. Andy was by far the best of Janice's husbands and boyfriends. He was a Vietnam vet whose occupation was cleaning out industrial chimneys. His crew would dress in hazmat suits and go on weeks-long jobs to different sites. He eventually developed cancer and died. He was pretty certain it was from Agent Orange exposure in Vietnam, where he'd been on a helicopter crew, but I'm not so sure. He also spent years cleaning waste chemicals off the inside of factory chimneys. That couldn't have been a healthy environment. But, in the end, it probably was just a genetic propensity.

Janice shifted to a caregiver role for Andy, then later became the decade-long caregiver for Louise as she slowly declined. She traveled around a bit after Louise died, and lived in Phoenix, Arizona, for a while, where her son had relocated. I think she enjoyed herself. Then she moved up to our house to help take care of Martha, who was in need of bladder catheterization for several months after her recovery from the heart attack and her ICU stay.

One can imagine Janice's life as a series of catastrophes and difficulties, but I think she was happy for the most part, and very glad to be of use to people. She certainly cut my hair innumerable times, for free, from when I was a child on into my college years. She had a deep capacity for loving and giving. She was also very kind to animals. Here is the eulogy I spoke when we buried Janice's cremated remains at Mount Olive Cemetery.

My first memory of my Aunt Janice is when I was a very little boy. She was standing outside the entrance to my grandparents' living room, and just peeking in. She said "Anthony" to get my attention. Anthony is what everyone was trying to call me when I was first born—it eventually became

Tony. I think she must have thought I was doing something cute and just wanted me to look up. I remember when I looked up seeing the beaming face of Aunt Janice. This is one of the first of all my memories in life.

I always carried that loving look with me through my life. No matter where I was, or what I was doing, I knew that Aunt Janice loved me unconditionally and completely.

That was the way Janice was. Very shy, until she felt she was secure. Completely loyal and loving. Always to be counted on. There were the big things. She raised my cousin by herself. She took care of a later husband as he became terribly sick and died. Then she and Mom took care of Mama Cooley in her old age. And when Memaw finally started feeling older, if she ever did, Janice took care of her to the very end.

But she was much more than a caretaker. Janice was an artist. She had the artist's sense of the beautiful. She spent a large part of her life as a hair stylist, often working for others, sometimes with her own shop. She was highly respected among the hair stylists she worked with as one of the best. She told me once how she liked to cut someone's hair several times so that she could find the way it grew—everyone's was different—and how to make it look best for that person. She was good at drawing and drafting when she was in high school, and she put this sense of the beautiful to the use all her life.

After Memaw died, she went through a very rough time, which she told me her dear cousins help get her through. But then she decided to fulfill some of her dreams. She moved to Phoenix, Arizona, farther out of the South than she'd ever been, and spent time with Chris, and while there she went for hikes and discovered the beautiful desert landscape.

Then, when Mom got sick, she pulled up stakes and drove across country to North Carolina. We'd been trying to get her to come up and visit since Memaw's death, but it took Mom and Daddy's illness to finally get her out. She settled in as their caretaker, and as with everything she did in life, she was conscientious and competent, and, very loving in taking on that task. She drove through the mountains on the way to

North Carolina, revisiting the Smoky Mountain beauty she had not seen since her youth, and had so loved then.

She and Mom spent many hours together, and she got to know my wife, Rika, better, and to know and love my kids. And they too came to truly love Aunt Janice.

When the end came so unexpectedly, she was with her family, her sister, and my family, and finally, at the very end, with her beloved cousin Betty.

There are so many memories of Janice I can share and we will, but the great memory I have of her is still the first: that loving, shy glance as she gazed at a very, very young me. A glance that made me feel safe and loved.

Martha was a mortgage underwriter for many years in Dallas, working for three or four finance companies, and for most of that period making about thirty percent more than Jerry in salary. Jerry, however, contributed to Hunt's retirement matching plan, and had a decent chunk of savings upon retirement. He'd grown to be liked by many in the company, particularly by its president, Ray Hunt. He was offered a comprehensive medical insurance policy upon retirement. This stood him in good stead during his decline, and Martha is included in it. In all ways, Martha and Jerry were far more comfortable financially in Texas than they ever had been in Alabama.

As of this writing, and after the passing of Jerry, Martha spends a great deal of time tending to my dog, reading, and gazing out the window at the trees in my backyard, where she also watches the squirrels and birds that cavort there. She goes on an occasional walk in the neighborhood, and is generally content.

I think the core of Martha Montgomery Daniel's personality was always her tiger-like devotion and advocacy for those she loved. This started with my great-grandmother, who was in many ways like a mother to her. She was fiercely loyal to Electa, and it was she who insisted Electa accompany the family on our longest and greatest Southwestern vacation. She literally pulled up stakes and moved back to Alabama to care of Electa in her final days. She was also devoted to Louise, but, at that point, Janice was available for help. Yet she made many trips from Texas to Alabama and back in Louise's final decade, usually driving the eleven hours it took.

Most of all, Martha was ferociously devoted to her children. She found the best schools she could for David and me. She pushed our teachers to pay special attention to us. She delivered us to innumerable music lessons, sports practices, youth group meetings, and Scout trips. She was there when we were sick, taking care of us. She was there at the doctor and the dentist and occasional hospital visit as we made our way through childhood.

Martha taught us to swim. Although I took lessons at the YMCA, it was really swimming with my mother at the University of Alabama Faculty Pool where I really learned to do it. She used to move off from the side and have me swim to her in the four-foot deep water (over my head at the time), always catching me just before I went under. I remember my true terror at going under, drowning. But I knew she would save me, if it came to that. I had not the slightest doubt I could count on her. I got farther and farther out, until one day—I could do it. I remember the smell of the chlorinated water, the flash of the sunlight. And I recall how she caught me up and hugged me in the water after I made it there and back, there and back, to her.

Most importantly, Martha saw to the mental, emotional, and spiritual development of my brother and me. She was not content with just any church, but sought out one with beliefs she could respect. She read to us constantly when we were young, and never once complained about all the reading I did (to distraction) as I got older. She liked the popular music of the day, and played it on the car radio constantly. She dragged David and me through innumerable museums, took us to plays and performances, and traveled with us to see wondrous sights. She was a wonderful, inspired mother in all respects. That was, perhaps, the role Martha was born to play, and she was brilliant in it.

Jerry

⤝⟫═◯◖═⟨⤞

Jerry Anthony Daniel (1940-2019)

I was with my father when he breathed his last breath and died. It was in a bed in a cognitive care nursing home in North Carolina. I saw immediately that he'd stopped breathing, and I leaned over and softly said, "Bye, Daddy. We love you." Rika, my wife, was with me, also.

While Jerry retained some level of awareness throughout his Alzheimer's Disease progression, I felt he was long gone in spirit by then. The last time we were fully together mentally was around 2007, just before he went in for a quintuple bypass operation on his heart. Not only did he survive the operation, he was up and walking within a week, and, two weeks after the operation, was walking a mile a day.

We lived in Allen, Texas, at the time, a suburb of Dallas. My parents had retired to Centerville, to their barn full of dogs. My mother stayed there to keep the dogs, and my father moved in with us to recover. It took him about a month and a half, then he was back to Centerville, and the dog care routine.

I had noticed some mental scattering before this time. I don't think the heart surgery had anything to do with the disease's acceleration, truthfully. It was going to take him, regardless. I think I first detected it around 2005 on a trip we took Out West. He was extremely talkative on that trip, and emotional, both uncharacteristic of my father till then. He was just sixty-five years old.

But after that, he felt the Alzheimer's himself. He began to make a series of recordings with a handheld voice recorder I got for him. They are a remarkable collection of memories, and great to spend an afternoon listening to. I highly recommend them.

Our final big trip together was a climb of Mount Blanca, a 14er in Colorado. 14ers are mountains that are over fourteen thousand feet above sea level. I believe my father and I climbed about twenty together, over the years. So far I've climbed thirty-three.

This was in 2010, and my father was not up for that climb. He was far weaker than I'd ever seen him. He was slow. The climb up felt interminable. And his mind wasn't working well. Nevertheless, we did make the summit, and had a wonderful time glissading—snow sliding—on the way back down. But I knew then that Blanca would be our last true mountain climb together.

After I moved to North Carolina, we went on a trip along the Blue Ridge and south of Asheville to look at waterfalls in Transylvania County. This was around 2013, and by that time he was so decrepit and out of it he had trouble walking a mile-long trail to some of the falls.

He got lost driving alone on the way back to Texas, and I had to talk him, turn by turn, out of Mississippi on the phone. I hoped that back in Centerville, my mother would look after him. What I didn't understand was that she had begun her own, less precipitous, mental decline. They spent a year and a half sinking into a terrible state. She was not only keeping thirty to forty dogs in kennels, she was feeding a huge group of local strays in several locations. Plus, she was bringing more dogs home.

Worse of all, the swelling of her legs brought about sores, and these became infected. I think my mother was probably running a low- to mid-grade fever for most of 2014. I checked in, but did not go for a really extended look-see until, finally, in November 2014, they broke down on the side of the road after my father accidentally filled his car with diesel fuel at a gas station. The sheriff couldn't get a straight answer from my mother on where they actually lived so that he could help them home. I suspect my mother was having a paranoid delusion that he might take her dogs if she told him where they lived. The poor guy ended up calling me for directions so he could arrange for them to get home.

At that point, I knew I had to come to Texas. It took me a week to make arrangements, then I drove down. In retrospect, I wish I'd gone sooner, but I had no idea just how bad things had become. They were in a terrible state, and so was the place. I took them to a hotel while I dealt with the barn and land as best I could.

With the help of a local vet, and about three thousand dollars, I put the dogs down humanely. I then scattered the horribly sick and maimed band of fifty or so feral cats my parents had also collected. There was no way to catch them.

By that time, my mother was delirious with fever. I didn't really know that's what it was. I thought she'd simply gone insane. In any case, I drove back as quickly as I could to North Carolina, for I feared that once I took her to the hospital, she was going to be there for quite some time. My father had also developed pneumonia—he was quite sick on the way back—but it would take another couple of weeks before this required his hospitalization.

So my mother went to the hospital first, and then my father. They would both end up there for about two months, including my mother's rehabilitation in a nearby recovery facility after she woke up from the coma she'd been in for three weeks. It was an extremely difficult period, and, when they came out of the hospital, I believed I was taking them home with me to die. The doctors agreed. They approved hospice care.

But my parents recovered, and my father lived with me another five years. My mother is still with us, weaker and older, but still basically going strong.

Jerry and Martha Daniel were an extremely resilient couple.

The saga of what happened with the Centerville barn and land would take its own tome, and I would be exceedingly depressed at the end of my account. Suffice it to say here that I eventually had it razed to the ground and burned.

But Jerry Daniel's life was by no means defined by its ending. Jerry was a small town kid. He spent some of his very early days in the country, and remembers going to a Randolph County elementary school. This was because Myrtice had moved back to live with relatives while Emmett was away during World War II. They lived deep in Randolph County, near a town—really more of an outpost—called Newell. Newell is in the north-central portion of Randolph County, about thirteen miles from the Georgia state line. Here is Jerry's extended description, from 2007, of the place and the time where he lived from 1942 to 1946, from the age of two to six.

This is about the town—it's really not a town . . . yes, it is a town—of Newell, Alabama, before it had a tragic ending one night when a 100-year flood flooded through and wiped everything out, the whole area: the bridge over the creek, the dam, the store, and the corn mill, and the cotton gin, and the hydraulic ram, and the post office, and old man's house who built things across the creek. Now we'll just talk about each one of these things.

The store was owned by Hanley and Iversen Lovvorn. They built a big store in Newell, and they had a post office. The store was a large building with a big porch across the front, and people from all over the neighborhood, all over the community, there came and told lies, and told stories, and traded news, and everybody talked to each other there about everything, about who knows what else. It was just a place to hang out.

There were a lot of different things there. And when I wanted to get a drink of water, or if a car needed water for its car radiator, or if they needed water to carry somewhere, or for any reason, there was a never-ending supply of water. It was pumped through a pipe from across the creek. The pipe was strung on the top rail of the swinging bridge that went across the creek. It came out and poured into a barrel by a big giant—probably about three- or four-foot diameter—sycamore tree. And water nobody used ran out—it was about an inch-and-a-half pipe—and it poured out into a big wooden barrel. The barrel had a hole in it near the top, and if nobody used water, it ran off, and ran into the ground back down to the creek.

But the pump was a hydraulic ram, which uses no electricity, just pressure from the water coming down the hill, to pump it over there. There was no water at Newell except at the barrel over there. So people would stop if they were driving through, and get a drink of water at the barrel at Newell, and stop and buy something at the store, even. Or walk across the swinging bridge, if they liked. As kids, we always went across the swinging bridge.

And across the swinging bridge, down below the dam about four hundred feet—maybe three hundred feet—there was an old man's house over there. The man lived over there, and he made woodworking items. He made fish baskets—which were about fifteen feet long and two feet in diameter—out of wood strips. And however many people wanted to buy them, he would sell them. The fish would go in, and the baskets had stakes cut with points on them pointing inward, where the fish would go in, but couldn't get out once they got in. And he also made canoes—well, not canoes. They were bateaus. They were square-end, wooden boats. If somebody wanted to hire him to build one, he'd build one for them. He charge about twenty-five to fifty dollars. Last time I talked to him, they were, I think, fifty dollars.

The store had bought one of his bateaus, and they always kept it up above the bridge in the mill pond created by the dam which supplied power to the corn grist mill, and the sawmill, that were both on the bank of the creek there. The bateau was in the mill pond, and the chain was loosely tied, just tied in a knot. Every once in a while, somebody would tie a bad knot and the boat would go over the dam, and you didn't have a boat up there until the old man had time to make another boat.

Anyway, there was always a boat up there. All you had to do was untie it. You didn't have to ask anybody, you just had to get it untied, and put it back. That was the honor system. You could go up the creek a little ways, probably about a quarter of a mile, and run into some rapids, and you couldn't get that heavy wooden boat over. So that stopped the boat that way, and the other way it went over the dam. So you were in trouble if you lost the boat, and let it go over the dam.

As kids, we went down there and took the boat and played in the water, and played in the mill pond, always being careful not to let the boat go over the dam, because we knew we'd really be in trouble if we did that. We'd have to stay away from down at the mill where the water ran in to turn the turbine. They called it the millrace, which was about a four-foot-wide segment of the dam which let the water come through and run over the turbine and turn the millstone.

The sawmill had a steel shaft running down the middle of

it. It had belts running over to each one of the machines that were for doing different things with wood, to the saws and the shapers and whatever they had. By the time I remember, or saw it, they had stopped using the sawmill. They invented better sawmills with gasoline engines, and it fell into disuse. But the corn mill was in use when I was a kid.

So it was two big, giant about four-foot millstones that turned in opposite directions. Or one might have been stationary, I don't know. I just remember one of them turned. And the water turned it, and it was free power, and the way you got your corn ground is that they would grind it by the basket. You had to bring a basket like if you wanted five baskets of corn ground up, you had to bring ten baskets so that you could give the miller a toll.

Then they would put five in the hopper, which he would grind when nobody was there, and while you were there, he'd grind your corn and put it in sacks, and give it back to you as cornmeal. So there was no money exchanged. Once, my grandfather said, "I'm going to the mill. I want to do about five baskets or corn, but I've got to take ten, because I've got to pay the toll." I don't know why they called it "toll," but that's what it was, they took a toll out: one half of the corn that you took down there.

So the cornmeal was one thing. It was about two hundred feet from the store, not very far. At the end of where the sawmill was, which was downstream from corn mill, between the corn mill and the store, it was about fifty feet over to the sawmill. The swinging bridge was down about fifty more feet. And there, of course, was the barrel and the store and the post office.

Across the road there was a cotton gin, and a cottonseed house where they separated the seeds out the cotton. They kept them. I guess they sold them. I think they ground cottonseed up into hog feed.

It was just kind of a do-it-all place, and you got your groceries in the store, and you got your gas out in front of the store. When I first remember the store, they had a pump there, it was a hand pump. You had to pump the gas up in the glass, a five or six gallon glass tank. Then, if you said you wanted five gallons, he'd put five gallons in there, and put the hose in, and pull the plug, and you saw your five gallons run out and into the car.

Back to the bateau. We would go get the bateau, and go up to the end of where you could get in the mill pond, the northern end. This was on Cohobadiah [Ca-HAH-ba-dah] Creek in Randolph County, Alabama. And probably about a quarter mile past Newell, the Cohobadiah ran into the Tallapoosa River. And between Newell and the Tallapoosa, about halfway, was this place we called the Indian Rock. It was a rock that protruded out from the wall of the hill there. It was like a slope-top carport. And underneath it had a place where the Indians had used to grind corn. So corn had been ground there, probably for hundreds of years.

All these things are still there, somewhere, if we could go down there, but the flood took all the buildings and remembrance of Newell. It's just not there.

There was a garage across the creek. There was a steel bridge there that was about six feet high, the banisters on it were about six feet high. It was probably one of the best bridges, pre-war bridges, that you could get. It was just a good bridge. But it did not hold up to the flood.

There was a big rock that was a swimming hole up from the mill pond, about a hundred feet. And on the weekends, all the kids, all the adults took kids and teenagers down to the big rock. At any time on Sunday afternoon, after church, of course, you could find about ten or fifteen people in swimming down there on a good hot summer day down there. Everybody was having fun jumping off the big rock, because it hung out over the water. I remember the first time I jumped off of it. It scared me to death. It was probably a twelve-foot drop. It was tough for me as a kid, the first time. Later on, we'd run up and jump off it ten or fifteen times a day. We jumped off backward, feetfirst, headfirst. You just had to watch out and not hit somebody down there.

We always talked about, "don't go too deep." You'd get stuck in the mud on the bottom. There was a layer of water there that stayed cold. I don't know, it was just a thermal. And I always stayed above that thermal, because it gave me the jitters to go below it in the cold water, which had leaves on the bottom, and a bunch of stuff. I did not like to go below that thermal that was in the bottom at the big rock. But now it's all gone, because the creek, when Newell washed away, the flood lowered the level of the water out there. The big rock is not a good place to go swimming. You can just wade in the water under the big rock now.

Iversen Lovvorn's house was about an eighth of a mile, two-tenths of a mile, something like that, up the road going to the east. And then, near the top of the hill, but not all way up to the top, the top of one little hill, then down and back up to the top of the big hill, my mother and I lived in a house there while my father was gone to the Army.

While he went overseas to Iran. We lived there from, probably, about '43 or '44 to '45. I don't know how long we lived there. I'll have to talk to my mother about that. But part of the time, we had a 1942 Ford. My father bought a new car before the war. He bought one of the last ones to be sold, because all the metal went to the war effort. So they didn't make Fords or any cars between 1942 and maybe like '45. I remember: '46 Fords, I think, were the next ones.

So my mother had a brand-new car. And due to the war effort, you were allowed five gallons of gas per month or something like that. I talked to my mother this morning and she said that she got enough by taking people around and getting their fuel allotments, she saved up enough gas coupons to go to Fort Leonard Wood. When my father came home, she went to Fort Leonard Wood in Missouri on her gas that she had got for her taking people and using their gas cards.

The cards were called rationing cards. Gas was rationed to everybody. Since she had a new car, she would take them places, and they'd give her coupons, and she'd saved some coupons and went to Missouri.

The man that ran the mill was Willie Stillwell. And Willie Stillwell was, I think he was at one time probably a minister, but he wasn't a minister when I knew him, but all his family was always religious. He always talked about religion. He wasn't kin to me, but he was my cousins', George and Barry, he was their grandfather. So we got a better tour of the mill. The mill was a three-story building with lots of things going on with that water power. It ran belts and things, it carried stuff upstairs, and this was an amazing building where the corn mill was.

I was with my grandfather once, I was spending the week with my grandfather, and he said, "we're going to go to the mill and get some corn ground."

So Monday and Tuesday, me, and my cousins, and my uncle Robert and my granddaddy, shucked corn. I think we shucked corn for about half a day, and the kids all got tired, and my grandfather left, and I think my Uncle Robert was given the task of finishing up the corn. I think we took about six or eight baskets of corn with us. We were going to get up and go to the mill the next morning.

My grandfather had a pickup truck, but he couldn't drive. But my Uncle Robert could drive. So when we got up and ate breakfast I said, "Granddaddy, can I ride in the back of the truck when we go to the corn mill?"

He said, "Jerry, we are not going to the corn mill in the truck. We're going to hook the mules up to the wagon. We're going to take the corn down there with the mules. So next morning we got up, and he hitch up the wagon to the mules, and the corn was loaded onto the wagon. We bounced off on steel wheels with a bumpy ride, headed to Newell.

There's a creek that ran through my grandfather's property, the creek was much bigger down the road about a mile or two, where we crossed it. So we were going downhill there, and I said, "Are the horses going to be afraid to cross the wooden bridge there?"

My grandfather said, "No, we're not going across the bridge."

I said, "What are we going to do?"

And my grandfather said, "I'll show you."

So just about a hundred feet before we got to the bridge, we made a sharp turn over the edge of the road, and down the bank. There was a road cut through there. The county had provided this road, but they probably maintained it only one time a year, or if it rained, they'd fix it, but people who had mules and wagons went down that way. And the reason wasn't because the horses were afraid—it wasn't horses, by the way, it was mules— the mules weren't afraid to cross the bridge. It was that they needed water. So you took the mules down there, and stopped them in the creek, and let them drink all the water they wanted.

Then we went up the hill to the other side, then down the hill to Newell. Crossed the Cohobadiah, and parked outside the corn mill, and everybody said their hellos. And four baskets were poured into the toll pile, and four were poured into the hopper that fed down into the grist mill. Later on, we got our sacks of meal. They were sacked up in five-pound sacks. We went to the store and bought a few things, went back home, and stopped by the creek up there again to get some water, never going across the bridge. We went back up the hill, and back up to my grandfather's house.

The only other thing that was at Newell was a school, which was west of Newell about . . . probably about half a mile over there, the school. And when the big flood came and washed everything away down at Newell, they didn't have a bridge for years, about two or three years. Anyway, that school is where I started school. In talking to my mother this morning, I said, "How long did I go to school at Newell? It seem like about, maybe, a month."

She said it was either a month or six weeks. And that is because my father had come in and told my mother that I couldn't go to that school up there, it wasn't good enough for me.

Jerry remembered going to school in Newell for those first few weeks of 1946, as well as riding into Anniston from Newell to begin at the school there.

My mother told me this morning that they wanted to transfer me to the Anniston schools, but those wouldn't take me because I didn't live in Anniston. They had a lot of trouble getting me in because we owned property, but hadn't paid any property taxes there. I think she paid forty dollars a semester, or something like that. She paid money for me to go to Noble Street School. But we still lived in Newell.

There were people who worked in Anniston and lived in Newell. It was about forty miles from Newell to Anniston, and people went up there to work. Every morning, my father and I got in the truck that was a carry-all. It was a Chevrolet. Or Dodge. Chevrolet and Dodge both made these carry-all trucks that looked like the SUVs of today with three seats in them, but these were utilitarian with real hard seats in them. I think there were two or three rows of seats in them. And I stood up between somebody's legs, between Daddy's and whoever was sitting next to him. And we rode forty miles to Anniston.

Jerry did have one core recollection of his school days in Newell. He mentioned it several times to me throughout his life.

When I first started school in [Newell, Alabama, in] 1946, on my first day, I almost didn't get water at ten o'clock in the morning because I couldn't make a paper cup. My cousin Rudolph came through with a bucket of water and a dipper from the well out in front of the school, and he said, "Everybody that can make a paper cup can have a drink of water. If you can't make one, you have to learn how." He took a piece of *my* paper and showed everybody how to roll a paper cup, and then he told me, "Jerry, if you want a drink of water, you have to learn to make one. You won't get water after today if you can't." So I had to learn how to make a paper cup to get water.

Here's how Jerry described the little school room.

The classroom had four sets of desks in the room, all facing the center. The first grade was on one side, and the second grade and the third grade were on the other, with the fourth grade looking back at the first grade.

Other times, there were girls out front on the porch, especially on rainy or cloudy days, who played jack-stones. They would throw the ball up, let it bounce once, and catch one rock, that is, a pebble that had come off the road that was there. And they had ten pebbles, they had ten rocks, and they would catch them. It was jack-stones. It was really jack-stones, but I think the game is called jacks, but anyway it was really, really hard to pick up ten rocks. I even tried it a couple times, and I couldn't do it.

When I later moved to town in Anniston and went to Noble Street School they had the little jingles, twenty stones, that were easy to pick up, to pick up ten or fifteen of those, if you had practiced with rocks.

And the boys went out and there were trails in the woods around the school, there around Newell. The boys mostly like to take a stick of stovewood and uses it as a steering wheel. We'd hold it out in front in our hands and run through the woods, and when you made a left turn, turn left with the stick, when you turn right, turn the stick right.

It was a poor school, and we didn't have a whole lot to play with down there.

One day I remember going home from school, and the school bus wasn't there to take us home, my cousins and me. We all lived in the same house at the time, so there were four of us: Bobby, Billy, Jack, and me.

We decided that we could beat the bus home. We started walking and we got down the hill, across the creek, past the country store, past the gin and the cotton mill, and the corn grinding place. Then we saw the bus coming down over by the gin, so we decided to hide in the ditch. We jumped in the ditch and laid down beside the road and watched the bus come down across the creek, by the store, and up the hill. And as the driver passed us, he stopped and opened the door and said, "Boys, get in this bus, and don't ever let me catch you trying to walk home again." So he dropped us off up the road about a tenth of a mile, at our house. We almost made it home walking, but we didn't.

Soon after Emmett returned from the war, the family spent about a year moving permanently to Anniston. That had always been the plan my grandparents were working toward from before the war. While they lived temporarily in Newell, my grandfather and father caught rides in to Anniston, where Emmett would work on building his shop or do electrical jobs, and Jerry would go to school.

By mid-1946, Jerry had begun to attend Noble Street School. My grandfather commenced to build Daniel Electric even while he worked at several iron and soil pipe foundries in town. As Jerry tells it:

> Talking about going to school at Noble Street . . . with the carry-all, or whatever you called those trucks back then, with the seats for a lot of people to sit in . . . so we rode to Anniston, and they dropped me off at school and, I assumed, dropped my father at 2800 Noble Street, where he was building the building so he could start his electric company.
>
> So we did that, and he did some work for the Anniston foundry companies, because he was back from the war, and things were booming, and they needed to make soil pipe [one of Anniston's specialties]. He was working for the Union Foundry most of the time, and sometimes he worked at the Standard and the Alabama Foundry.
>
> He went to work, and I went to school, then we'd get back in and drive back to Newell, forty miles. We did that until Daddy got the basement of his electric shop roughed in.

At first, the family lived below the shop on 28th Street and Noble. Or rather, Emmett built the lower apartment first, then built the shop on top of it. My father remembers that, for a while, the water line to the toilet was their only water supply. They would go to the bathroom in the nearby woods, and use the toilet tank for water.

> We had a plumbing line in, and had a commode. But we didn't use the commode yet because—strange thing—we didn't have any other water. We only had one line of water in, and the commode was in. I guess it was to have one appliance so you could get a water line turned on.
>
> It doesn't sound nice, but we never did think anything about it. We didn't use the commode during the day. There

were woods around the building up there where the electric company was. There were no houses there. My father, later on, built a house about twenty feet down from there. But at that time, there wasn't a house, and we would go out and pee in the woods. We saved the commode so we could drink the water out of it. That sounds yucky, but it was really safe.

Soon Emmett had the place completed, and began to work on the Daniel Electric shop above it.

Noble Street is Anniston's version of Main Street, and the downtown area is grouped along its path. They lived at the north end of town, up a steep hill. There were train tracks through town, and that area was literally on the wrong side of the tracks, socially. But it was a heck of a lot better than a hardscrabble farm in the Randolph County clay to Emmett and Myrtice. They never lived in Newell, Alabama, again, but Jerry never forgot the place.

I went to Noble Street School. As soon as we got able to, when we got a roof on, then my mother and I moved to Anniston. My father built an apartment down in the basement, and we moved to Anniston. I went to school at Noble Street School, and my mother didn't have to pay [a $40 fee] the next year, because we had paid taxes in Anniston.

And after that, I only went to Newell when I went to visit my grandfather in the country, or if there was some reason to go to Newell, and I did that for years. Then, when I learned to drive, I went back down to visit all the people in Newell that I knew.

Once when I was in high school, a friend of mine, Gus Glass, and I went to Newell. I don't know why we were down there. I guess just riding around because we had driver's licenses then. And we went down there, and I showed him Newell. We were sitting on the front porch of my cousins, and a group of two people in the neighborhood from up the road, my cousin and another person, were sitting there. Someone had called Anniston, had called the Army recruiter. . . no, it was not the Army, it was the Navy. They called the Navy recruiter, and asked him to come down and give them a test to see if they could join the Navy.

So my friend Gus and I were down there, and Gus was on the honor roll in all of his classes. So they came down, the recruiter came down, and he sat out on the front porch and he gave them a test. We were fixing to start the test, and the recruiter said, "Jerry, you want to take a test?"

I said, "I'll take it with you, but I'm not going to join."

And my friend Gus. His name was Bill. Bill Glass.

Bill said, "Give me one of those things, but I'm not joining either. I promise you, we're not going to join the Navy, but we'll take your test."

I later met Bill Glass when he was an adult. He had become a master-class operator of amateur shortwave radio. He had an amazing setup in the basement of his house that fascinated me. Bill Glass was also, I recently discovered, a second godfather at my Episcopalian baptism.

So we all five took the test. Two people passed it. Guess who they were. I didn't make the highest score, but I passed it, and Gus made, he probably made . . . I think he made a better score than anybody that recruiter had ever talked to, because he spent the next minutes trying to talk us into the Navy, telling him he could get him into flight school, he could get him anywhere and everywhere. But Gus wasn't buying that. He knew he was destined for something better than going into the Navy.

I drew a map last night of Newell so I could look at it and tell where things were. But it's all gone. It's not there, never to be again. And it was such a thriving little place. So much money made, and so many things happening down there. Washed away by the flood. I don't know when it was. I just went to my grandfather's once and they said, "Guess what, Newell washed away." We had to go down there and look at it, of course. Couldn't get across the creek because the bridge was washed away, so we kind of looked and it was just a pity. If it happened at night, nobody would be killed or drowned because there wasn't a house in Newell. It was just this town, with no houses. Even more of a reason to make it an unusual town.

✳ ✳ ✳

So the family lived *under* the shop in Anniston, the Daniel Electric office, in a basement apartment. The shop was built on a steep hill and was two-storied, although it looked like a one story building from the shopfront on Noble Street. Emmett and Myrtice then built a house next door on 28th. That was 5 West 28th, where Jerry mostly grew up— before the family's move in the late 1950s. They owned the lot next to 5 W 28th, also, on which Emmett built a storage warehouse for Daniel Electric, which housed supplies such as wire, conduit, and tools.

That little house would also shelter Ben Boalt's mother, Nora Creel Boalt Holsombeck (Myrtice's grandmother), and then Ben and Molly Boalt. After the family moved to Brighton Avenue, the apartment under the shop became a home for Patricia and Roger Dulaney for a time, and my cousin, Cindy, and her sister, Karen, as I've mentioned. Roger started his machining company on the porch down there, where he put his first lathing machine.

Not far down Noble Street, by the way, was Daniel Electric's principal competitor in later years, McLeod Electric, run by Buddy McLeod. My grandparents talked a great deal of dirt about Buddy McLeod's business practices and shoddy workmanship, but his daughter, Diane, and I went to school together and became great friends, best friends at times. We were never romantically involved, but I sometimes imagine how surprised my grandparents would have been if we had ended up married, perhaps combining our legacies to form an electrical contracting empire!

Anniston is a post-Civil War town built in the late 1800s and early 1900s. It was created because there was iron in the hills. There was unfortunately no coal nearby, as there was in Birmingham, and so the original smelters of the foundries had to be powered by charcoal. This was made from the forest on nearby hills, some of which became denuded. But they grew back. And some contained flying squirrels, as a result.

The area encompassing Anniston and Sylacauga and Talladega, Alabama, has a bunch of interesting soil characteristics. There are specific kinds of sand that can only be found there, and that are useful in construction and for certain ceramics. There is a sort of clay that's found almost exclusively in Anniston and somewhere in Italy. This clay made a couple of fortunes in town. Because Anniston was so recently founded, there was enormous attention paid, even when I was growing up there, to who belonged to the founding families. It was ludicrous.

The main Anniston founding family was the Nobles, but most of them had died out a hundred years later. Samuel Noble and his wife came from Rome, Georgia, where they owned an iron foundry, and created the town of Anniston from scratch. The town is named after Noble's daughter. Annie Noble. There's a great tomb for her in the city graveyard, topped by a twenty-foot-high angel. My old guitar teacher, Tommy Doss, used to sit under Annie's angel and write songs, back when I was taking lessons from him.

Other families, such as the Tylers and the Willets, all had descendants that I went to school with. My father went to Anniston High School, but I did not. My mother got me a partial scholarship to go to the Donoho School. It is the school where many of the rich kids in town go. I was not rich, however. I was one of the Golden Springs boys who were usurpers there. But I was a National Merit Scholar, and got a lot of academic accolades. I think Donoho got its money's worth out of my scholarship in using me for school promotion.

Little Jerry was most certainly not part of the Anniston ruling class, and neither were Emmett and Myrtice when they first moved to town. But eventually they would become solid citizens. Jerry spent the remainder of his elementary school years growing up at 28th and Noble Street. He became a small town boy, neither a country nor a big city boy.

Abutting Anniston was another fact of life for the citizens for many years. This was the U.S. Army installation called Fort McClellan. Fort McClellan had a bigger population than the town of Anniston itself during the war, when it handled much of the regional basic training. Beyond that, there were usually 10,000 troops there, and 1,500 civil employees. The Fort housed the Army chemical weapons school (eventually shut down due to international agreements on nerve gas and such), and much else. There was yet another major Army facility in nearby Bynum, Alabama, known as the Anniston Army Depot, or Anniston Ordinance Depot, earlier. This was the principal place for U.S. Army tank maintenance, repair, and refitting. The Depot is still going strong at this writing, and is a major employer in the area.

The reason the Depot existed, and that Fort McClellan continued to hum long after the big war, was because of a man name Bill Nichols.

He was the U.S. Representative to Congress for the local district. More importantly, he was the chairman of the House Armed Services Committee for decades. As such, he was one of the most powerful politicians in Washington. As long as Nichols was alive, the local economy was supercharged by these two Army installations, which he made sure got funded.

Bill Nichols dropped dead of a heart attack in 1989. Ten years later, Fort McClellan was shuttered in the Base Restructuring Act. McClellan had been threatened before, and Nichols had saved it, but this time they got it shut down. The decade after Nichols's death had seen it downsized repeatedly, and it was just a shell when they finally turned out the lights.

Anniston went into a spiraling depression, from which it took decades to recover. Bill Nichols' local chief of staff, by the way, was a man named Bob Hand, who lived down the street from us in the Golden Springs subdivision. His son David and my brother David were best friends when they were young.

Daniel Electric thrived for years by working jobs at Fort McClellan. The fort impacted Jerry's life in many ways. It provided his first independent job, for instance. Jerry, when he was eleven and twelve, was employed as a newsboy to deliver the local paper, the *Anniston Star*, to subscribers on the base. He learned how to fold the paper just-so in order to throw it neatly onto the front porches of the officer housing, he told me.

The job involved getting up long before dawn, arriving at the distribution point with a gang of other newsboys, and folding papers for delivery. The only adult involved in the operation, who was their overseer, would then load them all up in the back of a panel truck and drive them to the fort, where they would disperse, and distribute their newspapers. They would then reassemble and be driven back to town. Jerry would hurry along home, because he had a full day of school ahead of him!

But life wasn't all work for young Jerry. He and his friends roamed the neighborhood. There was a large open pit hole in the ground nearby, the John B. LeGarde Gravel Pit. Jerry and his friends played around the edges, and down in the pit when it was unoccupied on Sundays. And there was then-undeveloped Blue Mountain.

* * *

Going back to my earlier life when I lived in north Anniston 28th Street . . . there were a lot of kids around the neighborhood, and we all did things together. My next-door neighbors were a pair of twins who were a couple of years ahead of me in school. These were Gerald [1937-2004] and Jerry Timmons [1937-2008], and Jerry liked to climb the mountain. Blue Mountain was over about a mile over there from where we lived. You went up to the base the mountain. Later on we moved over there, on the edge of the very low part of the mountain over near Quintard Avenue. But we lived on Brighton, which is one street off of Quintard.

Before there was a subdivision up on Blue Mountain, we liked to go over there. Every Saturday morning it would be, "Let's go climb the mountain. Let's go climb the mountain." Anytime we couldn't think of anything else to do—"Let's go climb the mountain."

Jerry and I would go over there many times. He liked to hunt flying squirrels. There were flying squirrels over on the mountain. The trees were all the same height. At the time, I couldn't figure out why all the trees were about the size of the calf on your leg, and they were about twenty feet high. Every one of them on the mountain was exactly the same height and same size. Finally some old-timer around told me that the trees had been harvested for charcoal—Anniston is based on cast iron pipe, and they had smelters that made the iron for the cast-iron. They melted it with charcoal in the cupolas. They had clear-cut the mountain at one time just to make charcoal for the foundries in town. By the time we came along, the trees had grown back.

There were little short trees. The flying squirrels had been growing in them. They were little oak trees mostly, and if they got a hole in them, the squirrels could hollow them out, and they could live in those holes in the oak trees.

So we went what we called "squirrel hunting." And we were *flying* squirrel hunting. And, oddly enough, I haven't seen any flying squirrels in any other part of the country. We had a unique little spot that had flying squirrels on it. I have seen some at some Western parks, or they say they were there, but we regularly found flying squirrels. We would go find them. Jerry would hike up if I wouldn't go, and come back and say, "I got three this week."

Anyway, we would go kill flying squirrels if we could find them. The way we hunted the little things is we would walk up the mountain—the mountain had rocks all over the place— and if you found a tree with a hole in it . . . to catch the flying squirrels we had the mighty Red Rider BB gun. And we would take a rock and bang it on a tree if we saw a hole in the tree. And if nothing came out, we'd go find us a rock and beat on another tree. We would walk all over the base of the mountain, all around it, and up, until it got steep on the mountain, banging. Most of the squirrels were down around by the base. We would bang on the trees. The squirrels come out, climb up the tree. And—you've seen them—they have wings [of a sort]. And they would go down and come up and grab the next tree and go up it, and come down again. And we'd be running after them with BB guns, shooting them. And if you happened to hit one in the head it would knock him out, he'd fall down, and you could catch him.

I never did want to catch them, but Jerry always wanted them. He would do things like stretch them [after killing] on his fence and take their skin. He didn't know how to treat them, it never did work. But he loved to go up there, and I'd go with him as much as I could. When we would get tired of hunting squirrels, we would walk up to the tower which was on top of the mountain.

It was a wooden tower, a fire tower, and had a road that went up there. It didn't have a fence around it. Later on, they put a fence around it. But you could walk up to the top of the tower, and we would sit up there. If it was on a weekday, if it was in the summer on a weekday . . . the Army had some firing ranges. You could look down over the mountains see into Fort McClellan, to the firing ranges. They had artillery ranges, and they had places where . . . the Chemical Corps School was there, so they had places where they would . . . they had smoke generators that they would pull around behind the jeeps, and go out and put a bunch of smoke generators, and just cover a whole side of a mountain down there, one of those artillery ranges. They'd smoke the side of the mountains to keep the "enemy" from being able to see above the smoke.

Then, on other days, there would be target practice with mortars. They'd be on our side of the mountain, and you could hear "ca—choonk!" and hear a mortar come out. You could actually see the little black dot. The thing would go, and it would go out of sight, and you would lose them. We'd watch them flying through the air. Sometimes we could see them. We could always see where they landed.

And they had things out there that the Army had procured for some reason. I don't know where that got them, from things at the fort. They had refrigerators. They had the fronts of old cars.

Jerry played some sports, but Emmett was never really into sports, and didn't encourage him. Emmett did take an interest in Boy Scouts, and helped found a troop Jerry was a member of, awakening a lifelong involvement with Boy Scouts in my father.

There was a curious incident reported in the *Anniston Star* in 1950. It seemed the nine-year-old son of E.O. Daniel lit a match inside an oven filled with natural gas, and the resulting explosion engulfed him. Young Jerry was burned badly enough to be taken to the hospital.

This occurred in the house at 5 W 28th Street, when Myrtice was in the hospital delivering Sandy. A woman named Opal was staying with the family while she attended Jacksonville State University. She was doing babysitting chores, but she had not cooked in the house before. She woke up Jerry one morning and told him that she had been going to fix him biscuits, but she couldn't get the stove lit. Jerry took charge. He knew exactly how a stove worked. So he got a box of matches, opened the oven, and proceeded to strike a match to light the pilot. But the oven was filled with unburned natural gas.

The explosion threw him across the room, and into a wall. But the real damage was a burn to his face. He had closed his eyes in time to avoid damage, but his skin was crisped. It was bad, but relatively superficial. Emmett took him to the hospital, where he was treated and released without being admitted. Emmett did not tell Myrtice what had happened until Sandy was born, so as not to worry her.

But, as my father says, both he and his mother were in the hospital at the same time on that day. That was the way he remembered it.

My very first memory is standing beside my father shooting one of those toy bow-and-arrow sets, a blue and white one, with red stoppered arrows. I pulled back the bow and shot it at a small peach tree. My father had a larger, real archery setup, and he shot a real arrow, as well. I must've been around three years old at the time. I have no idea where this was, but in my memory we were at a hotel somewhere. Definitely not near home. On a trip. I have other impressionistic memories of when I was very young, and many of them involve him. I have a memory of climbing a steep hill, which I believe was in the Smoky Mountains, and holding onto saplings as we struggled up the slope. When we got there, I felt exhilarated, I remember.

Another impression I have is of our house in Alpine Hills, in Tuscaloosa. Several of the neighborhood kids were over, and it was pouring rain. We were all standing in the house's carport and trying to think of something to do. My father came out and announced we were going to play car. He gathered some yarn and some empty tin cans, with my mother's help. He then poked holes in the bottom of the cans and tied the cans around our waists, like little holsters. He took a pot and held it under the downspout of the house's rain gutter, and collected the rain. He put it into the cans that he had tied around our waists. We could then run around the carport's concrete floor as the water slowly trickled out through the holes in the can.

The object was to dash around as much as possible, then come in to get more water right before what was in the can ran out. We also were supposed to make car sounds. If you ran out of "gas," you had to stop wherever you were and wait. The last person who was able to keep moving and still have gas was the winner. I don't know if there were any winners, but it was a lot of fun to run around spewing water from a can tied around your waist, and having your dad fill it like it was a gas tank.

My father spanked me maybe three times in my entire life. One of them was so ridiculous that I remember it well. He had paid a hundred dollars—or rather, $99.95—to have his Mustang repainted, and was quite proud of the paint job. He'd just brought it home, and I was riding my bike around, looking at the new paint. The handlebar cover on one side of my bike had come off, and as I rode by to look, I dipped down and put a big scrape right across a portion of the hood of the newly painted Mustang.

Well, this was too much. When he saw the scratch—it was a pretty good gouge—Dad grabbed me and took me over toward the side of the car in order to get some room in the crowded carport to give me a spanking on the butt. But, as he lifted me up to spank me, he rammed my head into the side of the car and hit my front tooth there. I started wailing, and my mother began yelling, and I never did get a spanking. But I have felt terrible about it for the rest of my life, so I guess I provided my own punishment.

Jerry was always interested in cars, and going places, when he was a teenager. He and his friend Lee Cain had a couple of adventures in transportation that Jerry recounts in his 2007 recordings.

Lee Cain was my best friend in high school. In 1953, my daddy had bought me a 1952 125 cc Harley-Davidson motorcycle. Anniston was in a valley, and had drainage ditches running through town, through the valley, and they all ran into one big ditch that ran down the west side of town. And so you put all your things you didn't want on the west end of town, like foundries, and people who work in the foundries.

Lee and I used to follow the drainage ditches with our bicycles after a rain. We kind of wanted to see how much rain there was, what was flooding, what was not flooding, what was running fast, what was running through the drainage ditches—did it have trees coming through it, or trash, or whatever? And if the boxes washed out of a trashcan built up and stopped up a culvert somewhere, it would flood two or three blocks around. Anyway, we just liked to go and see how deep the water was, and what was flooding. We did that on our bicycles. Then, when I got my motorcycle, Lee and I decided we'd go and look at the drainage ditches.

So we went down the middle of Noble, down by the railroad tracks where the drainage ditch ran. We saw that. We went down to the far end of town where GE Supply used to be. GE wasn't there then. There was a cotton mill there. So we decided we'd go to Oxford [the sister-town abutting Anniston], see what was happening in Oxford, so we took off over to

Oxford. We got to Choccolocco, and the water went into Choccolocco, so we just kept going up the road, and went across Cheaha Mountain, by Horseblock Tower down there, on the east end of Cheaha Mountain.

And we kept going, and it started getting dark, and we got not knowing where we were, and we were just on roads where we didn't know which way we were going, or where we were going to come out. I started to get low on gas on my motorcycle. I didn't have any oil for my gas—because it was a two-cycle engine, we needed oil with the gas. So we came out on a highway, a really good two-lane highway. So we knew we were somewhere.

This was on a Sunday. We pulled into service station on the highway to get some gas. Between us I think we dug up thirty-five cents, which would buy us about a gallon and a quarter of gas. So we got thirty-five cents worth of gas, and we went out to the trashcan and dug through the trashcan. The gas cap on a Harley-Davidson had the amount of oil needed. They had told me at the Harley shop if you ever run out of oil, and you don't have two-cycle oil, you can just use thirty-weight oil. So we poured oil out of empty cans—you know, there'd still be some oil in there, and you'd get about a quarter of an ounce. Out of five or six, we got enough to get the oil filled up.

So we got the oil, and put it in the thirty-five-cents worth of gas. We asked the guy at the gas station which way was it to Anniston, and he said, "it's down that way forty miles, just follow the signs."

So we went down the road. We came out at Hollis Crossroads, and I knew where I was. We turned left, and went up and over the mountains, and back around to home, on my thirty-five-cents worth of gas. I was relieved. I knew we were going to make it then.

Anyway, that was our little excursion. We overlooked watching the water run in the ditches.

Later on, Lee and I bought a 1932 . . . what the guy told us was a 1932 Chevrolet truck. The body was in pretty good shape, the bed, but the seat springs were poking out, and the window was rusted and wouldn't go up and down. We bought it for fifty dollars.

I thought we bought it for thirty-five, but I talked to Lee last Christmas, I called him, I hadn't talked to him for forty years, and I called him, and I said, "this is a voice from forty years back." We bought the truck for fifty dollars. Actually bought it for forty-nine dollars, because the guy gave us a dollar's worth of gas. So we bought the truck for forty-nine dollars, and we parked it on the hill by the house at 5 West 28th Street, which was a very steep hill.

We could occasionally get the truck running. We played with it, and we got it running. We knew it would run. We wanted to get the head off to see . . . it wasn't an A- or T- Model motor. It was a V-8. And everybody told us that Chevrolet didn't have a V-8 until 1938, and they didn't sell one until 1954. But we were told it was '32 Chevrolet. I don't know what it really was. Lee and I still argue about what it was. He said it was a Ford, and I say it was a Chevrolet. I found a picture of one in a magazine down here in the country, a picture of a '32 Chevrolet truck, and they only made about five hundred of them, so I don't know if that's the one we had, or if it was a Chevrolet or a Ford. Lee said it was a Ford when I talked to him last Christmas.

The interesting thing about the truck was that we wanted to get the heads off, and it had an aluminum head on it, which seems strange for a '32 automobile to have aluminum heads. We had gouged them, and scratched them, and done everything to get them off. The best we could come up with it was that it was aluminum, it wasn't steel, because we couldn't have scratched steel. So we had the truck, and we couldn't get the heads off. We took all the bolts off. That was our plan. We got all the bolts off the heads on the truck. We loosen them up about an inch. We decided that we would roll down the hill and get it running—it wasn't any problem, we'd done that a number of times—and we would go down the hill and get it running, then put it in reverse and gun it, and go back up the hill, and that would blow the heads off, the compression on the engine would blow the heads off, one of them, at least, and we could see what was in there.

The end of the road was Russell's house by then [Russell Albert Stevenson, Jr.]. They had moved from up at the ballpark down to the end of our street. Anyway, we got down to the bottom of the hill, put it in reverse, gunned it back up the hill as fast as we could go backward, and looked at it. Nothing had come off. Nothing. So Lee and I said, "Okay, we can't get a head off this car."

So, anyway, a guy came by and wanted to buy the wheels off of it. He asked me if I'd sell him the four wheels off of it for $35. I said, "I don't know, I'll have to ask my friend, Lee, who owns half of it, if he wants to sell it. But we don't want it sitting out there without any wheels on it."

So I went over to Lee's and said, "A man wants to buy our truck for $35. He doesn't want to buy the truck, he just wants the wheels on it."

It had wire wheels on it, which was a thing in demand at the time for old A-models and T-models. And these were thirty-six-inch wheels, and they had thirty-two-inch wheels on A-models.

Lee said, "Let's see if he'll buy the whole thing for fifty, and we'll get our money back."

I told the man, and he said, "I've got to talk to my partner about that."

Well, he came back with fifty dollars, and bought our forty-nine dollar truck. So we made a dollar off of our truck. And it was gone, never to be thought about again, until I saw this picture in a magazine that looked exactly like that truck. Lee says it was a Ford. I said, "The guy told us it was a Chevrolet." But Lee said, "Yeah, but I've talked to him since, and he said, 'Really it was a Ford.'"

So I don't know if it was a Ford or Chevrolet or what, but we made a dollar off of it, and we had a lot of fun with it. It ran. But all we wanted to do was get the heads off.

When Jerry was an older teen, he frequently borrowed Daniel Electric vehicles to drive. While his parents were hard on him in many ways, he was also the favorite son of the company, and he was able to use all the equipment and vehicles that they possessed. He also had that little blue Harley that he greatly enjoyed riding around. I think he still had that after he got married, at least for a time. I vaguely recall seeing it during my very early childhood.

Jerry spent his toddler years mostly in Newell, Alabama, in Randolph County, and often visited to hang out with his cousins after he moved to Anniston. They played a great deal in the creek that ran near the Newell store, and eventually fed into the Little Tallapoosa River, the main river drainage of Randolph County. This was Cohobadiah Creek. Later, when he was the Scoutmaster of Troop 9, he took the troop down the Little Tallapoosa many times on overnight canoeing trips. We camped on sandbanks, and in cornfields along the way.

The Little Tallapoosa was filled with reddish water, which came from the red clay of northern Randolph County. Where the river enters the big Tallapoosa River, the confluence looks like blood flowing into a brown slurry.

I think he and the troop even took the canoes down Cohobadiah Creek one time, but not with me along. As he chronicled decades later, the Cohobadiah experienced a large flood, and the old buildings of Newell were wiped from existence by the rising waters.

But once when he was playing with his cousins, they came across what my father called the biggest snake he'd ever seen. It was as big around as an adult arm, and was maybe twenty feet long. It was a water moccasin, the most dangerous snake of the South. Extremely poisonous. He and his friends began chasing the snake, and firing at it with BB guns that they had along. This angered the snake, and it charged after them. Moccasins are very territorial.

They all ran away. But over time they hunted it, and finally cornered it. Water moccasins generally stay in the same area. They shot it, and pelted it with rocks, until it died. They then carried it back to the road, the biggest trophy they would ever acquire.

I think that this incident was one of the things that turned my father against hunting. He was not philosophically opposed to hunting, by any means, but he never got into it as a sport. Emmett *was* philosophically opposed to it, didn't do it at all, and didn't teach Jerry how to do it. But most of Jerry's cousins in Newell were hunters, and he might've acquired the skill, had he wanted to.

There was a time when we fished a great deal. I think it was more because my father got interested in the technology of the bait and tackle, than any desire to catch fish. This was one of the many enthusiasms that we went through during family weekend activities of the 1970s. My mother participated, as well. After a while, we gave up fishing, and never did it again, but, because of that, I do know, in general, how to fish.

Jerry quickly adapted to being a city kid. One of my father's favorite anecdotes, which I heard more than once, was the story of being taken to elementary school in a taxicab.

Okay, here's another story about Noble Street School. And this one, Martha makes fun of me every time she hears it. Here's what happened. Daniel Electric had started, and it was going, and my mother became more and more of a part of it. And, as she became more of a part of it, she had to pay other people to do things that she normally was doing. And she had the money to pay them, because we needed to keep the company going. We had people that came sometime, but not regular. She did later, when we moved to Brighton, we had a maid on Thursday, every week. Occasionally she would hire a maid.

My mother and daddy didn't like me to walk to school—it was six blocks from 28th to 22nd Street, where the school was, along Noble Street. So somebody said, "Well, why don't you get a taxi to take him?"

So this old taxi driver agreed. I think he just came by the shop and asked her if she would do it.

So, for a long time—I don't know how long—the taxi driver . . . the old man was so nice, he gave us presents for Christmas—he would come and pick me up, and then he would go up the road and get Gail Cagle, who lived up the road, and we'd go across the little hill there, and pick up somebody else, and back down to McArthur, and pick up somebody. Then, when the taxi was loaded, we would go down. He had a fare for a dollar a day. . . no, it cost her a dollar a week, back then. So she paid him one dollar every week, and he picked me up, and those other kids, and we all knew when he was coming. He was always sitting at the gate at the fence in front of the school. He was always there. So I didn't have to walk to and from school at Noble Street after Daniel Electric got going.

Martha had to ride the bus. She had to get on the bus, and ride the bus all the way to downtown Birmingham to go to school. She used to get so mad at me, because I got to ride in a taxi going to school. Don't mention this to Martha. She doesn't even like to hear the story.

I think Jerry had a tougher time of it in junior high and high school, and this was probably the happiest memory of his schooling. I suspect he later discovered the intense social pecking order of Anniston society, and that he was not on one of the top roosts in the chicken house. I always had a broader perspective on Anniston, thanks to Martha and Jerry, and, even as a teen, I found the intense status struggles in that pretentious small town completely ridiculous.

As the Daniel family began to grow larger, with Patricia, then Sandy, and then Ricky, Emmett acquired the land and built the house on Brighton Avenue, in a new subdivision on the side of Blue Mountain in Anniston. This area is to the east of Noble Street by a mile or so, across Quintard Boulevard, the large road that parallels Noble Street and is the biggest traffic artery in town.

The Brighton house was built toward the end of Jerry's high school years, when he was seventeen and eighteen. I think they moved in 1958, so Jerry didn't live there long. Yet it was built exactly where he and Jerry Timmons had used to play in the woods, so he was long familiar with the area. In fact, it was built directly on one of the old pits where the charcoal for the foundry had been made. Jerry knew this because he'd seen it from above, and heard the process described by an "old-timer," as he put it. The biota in the ground evidently was destroyed by the process for at least several decades, because Jerry said they never could get anything to grow in the backyard of the Brighton house.

Blue Mountain, the geographical feature, abutted Fort McClellan's boundary. On the other side of the mountain was an Army practice area and firing range. The fort is very near to the town. I grew up listening to shells drop, and machine guns fire, throughout my teen years in Anniston.

While he lived on 28th Street, Jerry and his friends frequently crossed Quintard Boulevard and climbed the mountain. They often looked down into the fort property. It was fenced, but there were ways through. There were many sorts of mangled Army machines down there, plus items like old refrigerators and such, that were used for Army target practice. And there were a great many unexploded shells lying about. My father never ventured onto the fort property. But one boy in his neighborhood did. This was Russell Albert Stevenson, Jr.

Later on, we had a friend, a new neighbor. We had a baseball field in our neighborhood. It was two empty lots that were up the alley from my house. So we had a baseball field out there, and they built two houses in it, and took away our baseball field. So we didn't really [at first] like the people who lived in the houses. But anyway, a truck driver from Pennsylvania moved up there, and he had a son named Russell.

We liked Russell. We took Russell to the mountain, and we always, Jerry and I, always stopped at the fence to Fort McClellan. We were afraid to go over there because they might be shooting mortars. When they shoot mortars, you don't know where those things are coming. Or if there are unexploded ones. Because we'd hear some go over and not see it hit. We knew it went, and it didn't go off. When Russell moved in, we took him up to the tower and let him watch all this stuff.

And . . . he was kind of a weirdo. He was into everything that was *dangerous*. Russell would go over and climb under the fence, and go into Fort McClellan. And one day he came home with a knapsack full of unexploded mortars.

I said, "Russell, get those things *out* of here! I don't even want to *know* about these things!"

He said, "Nah, I'm going to keep them."

Anyway, he kept them around, and he examined them. I don't know, maybe he took them apart. I was scared he was going to kill himself. But there were lots of reasons he was going to kill himself.

One of his favorite things to do was to get all the kids in

the neighborhood to run up to the store, our little local store, and get a piece of cardboard. He'd cut a box up, make four pieces of cardboard for people to hold. He would break the points off of his arrows, and shoot arrows up in the sky, and you had to catch them with your piece of cardboard. This is the kind of thing Russell thought was really neat.

As he grew older, there was an empty lot across the alley from his house, and they had a bulldozer up there. One time he came to us and said, "Let me show you something. I found out that they don't lock these tractors up over here. You can crank them up!"

And I thought, oh no, we're going to get in trouble over this.

We went down there, and he cranked it up and made it go "rrrnnn, rrrnnn, rrrnnn." And we saw a light come on in the neighbor's house, and we all took off running and left Russell out there.

He shut the tractor off, and came and found us. But, anyway, he was always into some kind of trouble. Into something that would *cause* trouble.

Once, before the tractor incident, I went out in that vacant lot with him and he said, "Let me show you. I can build a fire this big, and put it out with just one bucket of water."

And he'd built a fire in about a twelve foot circle. And then took a can and sprayed the water over the fire and put it out, but we could have burned some houses down there, he could have. I didn't do that. But I didn't even want to *know* about the things that Russell was into.

And then he got hold of some carbide. He was making acetylene gas with his carbide. He wasn't getting enough smoke out of it, so he blew on it, and he blew on it. And it ignited, and he burned his face. He looked like an Indian for a while.

I had burned my face, and I knew what it felt like. When either Ricky, my brother, or Sandy, was born—I don't know, I think it was when Ricky was born, maybe—I'd had my face burned when the maid came in, when my mother was at the hospital, she got the maid to come and cook breakfast for us, and get us off to school. She came in and said, "Jerry, I can't get this one to light in here. I was going to make y'all some toast."

And I said, "All you have to do is strike a match and hold it over this little hole in the bottom of the oven."

I went and struck the match and—boom! It knocked me over, and my face . . . I had squinched up my face because I knew it was blowing, and it left creases where I didn't get burned. I looked like an Indian with warpaint on.

So I knew that his face was hurting.

So anyway, that time my mother and I both were in the hospital. I was in the emergency room, and she was in having, I think, Ricky. I am not sure, but anyway, back to the mountain.

Russell went up there and found, besides the refrigerators, and cars, and Army Jeeps, and anything the Army could pull out there to use for targets to blow up on the side of the mountain—which [by the way] was not the mountain we were on, it was a mountain next door—he'd found some slot machines.

Jerry was not done with Russell Stevenson yet, however.

What was Russell doing the last time? He was cranking the tractor up? Burning the fires out in the woods? These were weeds that were higher than our heads, not little bitty fires. He just wanted to show us that he could do it. It scared me to death, because I was out there, and I wasn't burning the woods. The neighbors called the police, and we could see them coming up on Noble Street. We were about fifteen to twenty feet below Noble Street. We just hid in the bushes and walked out, got away from there.

Russell was always trouble. The most unique thing about Russell was he collected comic books. Russell collected comic books, and he was an EC comic book collector. He probably had every EC that was ever made. Anything that he could ever get his hands on, if it was an EC, then he would buy it.

And then a magazine came out, and he bought the number one issue of it. It was called *Playboy*. And he collected ECs and

Playboys the rest of his life. But his life was not going to be very long.

He experimented with everything. He did all kinds of things. Back then, we didn't have drugs or anything like that, but he experimented with—what's the stuff that makes acetylene lamps, carbide—he had carbide, and he'd throw it in water and watch it spew and lighted it on fire. He burned his face, and then what else did he do?

I don't know, but one night this friend of mine and I came back from a football game in about the eleventh or twelfth grade in high school. And there were cars and police cars all around Russell's house down there. So we go down there and ask, "Hey, what's happened here?" People said, "We can't tell you. Police told us not to tell anybody."

Well, what had happened was that Russell had shot himself.

I knew he had these bullets with the ends cut off of them. And he had put what he thought was a blank in, evidently. Or he might've been playing Russian roulette for real. Who knows about Russell? Anyway, he had put what *they* said was a blank in this gun, and twisted it, and pulled the trigger, and it blew his brains out all over the living room ceiling.

So anyway his parents lived down there with the bullet hole up in the ceiling for three years, and then I think I went away, I don't know. They left, but they never did even cover up the hole where the bullet went in the ceiling up there after he shot himself. Anyway, that was Russell's story.

In high school, Jerry became interested in art and drawing. It became clear that he had talent, and he developed that skill further with a sympathetic teacher at Anniston High School. He also at that time had a part-time job helping clean and handle equipment with an area dance teacher, the imposing Zenobia King Hill. I'm not sure how he got the job. His recount of it makes it seem that "Miss Zenobia," decided to hire him without his bothering to apply. She informed him and a friend that they would be working for her, and that was that. Hill's imposing personality—from the way Jerry described her, she was a veritable small-town Twyla Tharp—had a big effect on him, and probably directed him even more toward respect for the arts.

He took drawing courses at Anniston High, and I believe he took more drawing courses at Jacksonville State, as well, and became quite the draftsman. In March of 1958, he even had a showing of his drawings with several area students at the Anniston Natural History Museum, then called the Regar Museum, which was written up in the *Anniston Star.*

Jerry's drawing talent was no doubt a reason Emmett and Myrtice decided that Jerry was going to be an electrical engineer. He might even have followed their wish had they not acted as if the decision was made and he had no choice.

I'm not sure Jerry knew what he wanted to do at first. I think his greatest ambition in his late teenage years was a vague desire to become a helicopter pilot. He had joined the Civil Air Patrol, and really enjoyed the activities. He loved the idea of combining the outdoors with his fascination with technology. He went to a Civil Air Patrol camp in Montgomery his senior year of high school. It was my mother's junior year at Phillips.

And there they met.

They encountered one another at a mixer of all the CAP kids doing the camp. After that, he began going over to Birmingham to see Martha during her senior year of high school. Jerry himself was at Auburn University at that point, for a somewhat disastrous year.

He went there because his parents wanted him to. They'd heard it had the best electrical engineering program in the state. They were paying his way, I believe. But he was not happy there. Mainly, he just wanted to drive to Birmingham and see Martha. That summer, the summer of 1959, he and Martha decided to elope to Georgia and get married.

I'm not sure what he was driving at the time. Probably a vehicle he'd borrowed from Daniel Electric to take to Auburn. So they drove to Trenton, and arrived late at night, as my mother tells it, where they were married. After that, they moved in together, but I'm not sure where they lived. They decided that they would try various places to see what and where they wanted to end up in life. And I think it was not much longer after that that they moved to Tampa, Florida.

During the early 1960s, my mother was introduced to the Daniel extended family. She came to really like my grandmother's mother, Ruth Whitmore. And she liked Rior Jane Daniel, my grandfather's mother, as well. At that point, my mother says, my grandmother Myrtice was more kind to her than she was later. I would not be surprised if my grandmother, for some random reason that my mother had no control over, decided my mother wasn't worthy of Jerry. In any case, what started out as a fairly amicable introduction into the family eventually went sour. Knowing them, I can say with some certainty that whatever happened was undoubtedly my grandparents' doing. It must have taken quite an effort to alienate my mother, who was always loyal to a fault, and given to respect family, but they managed to make her thoroughly dislike them.

I'm not sure how Martha and Jerry occupied themselves in Tampa other than work, but I know that Jerry drank his first legally acquired adult beer there when they visited Busch Gardens. He told me he had to prove that he was old enough to drink. They also attended a jai-alai game. Eventually they left and came back north to Tuscaloosa, where Jerry got a job drafting, and enrolled at the university.

Jerry's grades had been fine, but not great, in high school, and were disappointing at Auburn, but he went back to school with a vengeance when he got to Tuscaloosa. He did well at Alabama. He was a couple of years older than the typical entering students by then, so he had a maturity beyond their years. He was particularly good at math, and probably would've been a math major, but he had an advisor he didn't like who made him repeat a course from Auburn that was far beneath his current abilities. He thought it was a total waste of time. Jerry ended up majoring in geology, with a math minor. I've seen some of the drawings he did for his geology classes. They were beautiful cross-sections, works of art in themselves.

Drawing was never far from Jerry's heart. In the mid-1970s, for about three or four years, my father created a Christmas slide show that was the wonder of my neighborhood. I don't know where he got the idea, but Dad drew up a set of slides that told the Christmas story with illustrations and captions. He made the drawings himself. They were modernist depictions, simple and powerful little sketches in a few bold strokes of primary colors. He had slides made of these with a black background. This resulted in the slides having an almost neon quality when projected, yet not garish in any way. It was a beautiful, elegant set of drawings.

He made these slides in Tuscaloosa, I believe, using resources at the U.S. Geological Survey drafting department. But the first time I remember his using them was in Anniston. He put in two poles in our front yard and stretched a sheet of white plastic of a certain sort between them. Then he set up his slide projector to shine from a basement window. From there, he rear projected onto this sheet in our front yard. The result, at night, was spectacular. The images were about as large as a garage entrance, and our slide projector was powerful enough to make them crisp and bright.

Dad hooked up the projector on a homemade timer he created. He took the electric cord to the projector change button, cut it open, and spliced one wire to a big clock laid on its back. The clock had a sweeping second hand. To this, he affixed an electrical connector at thirty second intervals on the clock face and one on the second hand. He wired the projector changer into this contraption. So, twice a minute, the sweeping second hand of the clock struck an electrical contact and signaled the projector. Dad also—and I can't remember how he did this—had the projector slide tray wired up to reverse itself after the slides were done and start over. This was a straight tray instead of a circular one.

This produced a show outside of about fifteen images that cycled every thirty seconds and depicted the Christmas story and a few extra Christmas images he'd drawn, such as an Advent wreath. He turned it on after dark every night starting about the beginning of December. And this was our Christmas light display for the year.

People lined up in cars nightly to see this. We used to have a line down the block some nights. They would sit and watch the whole slide show through, then drive away and let the next person watch. About two to three cars at a time could view it.

Dad tinkered with his set up, of course. He and Mom got a Christmas album and put a standard stereo speaker outside the basement window that played Christmas music as loud as they could crank it—which was not very loud when heard from the street, but effective.

The Daniel Christmas slide show was a spectacular success. We did it for several years until, I think, some grumpy neighbors inevitably complained, and Daddy got bored with it anyway, and moved on to new projects.

My father loved to make slides. We couldn't afford a professional camera back then—they were prohibitively expensive—but he did get a camera that could make 35 millimeter slides. We had slides from our Out West vacations, and slides of our Washington, D.C., and Disney World trips. He made careful photos of wildflowers he found beautiful, and many sunset and landscape shots. They were all expertly composed. Watching one of my father's slide shows was never a burden to me, even as a kid.

My parents went through many enthusiasms during the 1970s while I was a youngster and a teenager. For a while, they became interested in horse shows. This was mainly my mother's interest. We went to many horse shows, and watched the English saddle riders take their large horses through the paces. We never contemplated buying a horse. We just watched. I'm not sure what Jerry and Martha got out of it, but they certainly dragged me and David to a bunch of them.

That interest then transmuted into going to mini-bike races. There is an entire summer where every weekend we went to a mini-bike race and watched young kids on motorcycles race around a dirt track. This, in turn, became an enthusiasm for bicycles and bicycle motocross racing around dirt tracks. Then, like a door shutting, this activity disappeared and we went to no more.

The major activity of my younger years, however, was going to weekend craft fairs. We went to dozens of these over the years. At these, we'd set up a booth using our foldout aluminum camping table. My mother and father covered this with an old sheet or a quilt. Then my father would set out his wares.

What he had to sell was a map. It was a map of Alabama as it was in 1823. He'd made it painstakingly from a couple of maps he found in the U.S. Geological Survey archives in Tuscaloosa when he worked there. It was not a copy, but an interpretation, an adaptation, of those old maps. He sold his Alabama 1823 map reproductions by themselves. But the big ticket item, what he was really selling, was one of these maps mounted on an old piece of wood. These Jerry would carefully prepare.

He'd had the original map multiply printed on a yellowish parchment paper. He would burn these copies around the edges (this was where I got to help out; I loved doing this with a match). Then he would glue them to old barn boards, or to wooden shingles from old houses. These he would decoupage to a high gloss.

Alabamians love these things. They bought them to decorate their dens, living rooms, and offices. We sold many of them over the years.

After a while, he also added a map of Benton County to the collection, which is what Calhoun County used to be before the Civil War. In the beginning years of our craft show adventures, he also sold keyrings and rings that he had carved from peach seeds. He always loved peach seeds, and was fascinated by their crenellations. He would finish these bits of jewelry to a high gloss with lacquer. And he would also create that great staple of 1970s hippie jewelry, the spoon ring. These he made from old sterling silver spoons he picked up here and there. My mother had one of these rings that she wore for years. Anyway he shaped them with a portable blowtorch and sold them, along with the peach-pit rings, and peach-pit keyrings. He sold these side-by-side with the maps for a while, but eventually he only sold the maps and boards. We did this for maybe six or seven years. My favorite craft fair was the annual one at DeSoto Caverns in Alabama. I got to go into the caves when we went there. In general, I didn't have much to do at the craft fairs, so I got to run around, usually at a state park or a city park with a playground, and do whatever I wanted.

This was also when I encountered my father's utter lack of interest in actually making any money. He would sell the maps for a song if he detected that someone didn't quite have enough to buy one of his mounted masterpieces, but wanted it badly. He would knock the price down and basically give it to them. My mother tried to get him to build selling the thing into more of a business, but he never really put his heart into doing that. In the end, Boy Scouts arrived, and took over our weekend activities. It subsumed the craft fairs, and we stopped going. But I still have the original copy of Alabama 1823 hanging in my living room above the fireplace.

There are a great many stories about Jerry Daniel and the Boy Scouts that I could tell—it was a large part of his middle years—but it would take practically a book in itself to recount the whole adventure of my father with the organization. He started out as an adult volunteer in Troop 9. The original founders of the troop, which included contractors he had worked with professionally and didn't particularly like, were unable to continue for one reason or another. After that, the Scoutmaster role was taken by a northern fellow, a retired Army colonel. I was a patrol leader under him, and then an assistant senior patrol leader. He and I nearly came to blows once or twice. Let us just say that I did not respond well to his method of leadership. His son graduated, and they moved away, and the Scoutmaster role fell upon my dad's shoulders.

So Jerry became the Scoutmaster of Troop 9. His good friend Cleo Tibbets became the assistant scoutmaster. Cleo's son, Roger, was a close friend of mine.

My father and Cleo remained good friends for many years. They only fell out of touch after my father moved to Dallas. I believe that Cleo got sick and died at a young age. I kept in touch with Roger for a number of years, but also eventually lost contact.

My father really enjoyed being Scoutmaster. He did a great job. Boy Scouts is about leadership and camping, but for a boy, it's truly only about camping. Scouting is a boy-led operation in theory, but what the adults can and will do is necessarily a big influence on what the troop is able to do.

Jerry put to work his knowledge of geology. We went on a couple of epic geology campouts all around Alabama, digging for fossils, climbing on road cuts, and going in caves. At the Lost Sea Cavern in Tennessee we stayed overnight in the "wild," undeveloped portion of the cave. We had wilderness survival campouts down on my grandfather's eighty acres in Randolph County. In fact, Troop 9 had multiple campouts there over the years. We also used the eighty acres as a fundraising source for the troop.

Jerry, Cleo, and several boys would go down there, cut a tree or two, and we would split these up for firewood. We would sell the firewood by the truckload to raise funds for Troop 9.

The eighty acres was also our family firewood source after we added a chimney and fireplace to our house at 1509 Cloverdale Road, in Anniston. My father, David, and I built that chimney by hand. I remember many times riding with my father in his heavily loaded blue pickup truck from the eighty acres, the truck weighed down with oak and hickory we'd felled and split. I became an expert with a chainsaw, ax, chisels, and maul under my father's tutelage. I could drop a tree exactly where I wanted, and later proved it a couple of times, once impressing my father-in-law in Spain by cutting down an enormous pine tree to fall precisely away from the side of his house and into a driveway for cutting up. I later quartered and split the whole thing for their use (this was very difficult, because the tree was pine). He was pretty impressed. I owe my skill in that regard entirely to my father.

For several years, Troop 9 produced a haunted house at Halloween for a fundraiser, something that Cleo Tibbets really loved to put together. But the thing got so spooky that the church asked us not to do it anymore, so we had to stop that activity. All the boys really enjoyed it, and my father made it extremely gruesome with one special effect he created. The scene was of a monstrous mad scientist who was cutting someone's legs up with a machete. The doctor and patient were both played by scouts. The doctor cackled and the patient screamed.

Jerry made a sturdy table, then sabre-sawed a hole in it so that the patient-scout could dangle the lower portion of his legs down through it, bending them at the knee. This was covered by a sheet, and we had some beef bones that my dad had gotten from the grocery store butcher extending out from under the sheet and going into some boots. The other scout who was playing the mad scientist could whack away on those beef bones with a machete or hatchet, and it would seem he was chopping into the patient's lower legs. It looked entirely realistic. That was probably the one that got the church to shut the thing down, actually. But it was fun while it lasted.

We also went on many hikes and regular campouts of various sorts. After I became old enough, I was elected as the senior patrol leader for two years. I planned as many interesting campouts as I possibly could get away with.

We also did these wild weekends called Combat Campouts. We would fill small brown paper sacks with flour, then go out into the woods and throw them at each other. If you got hit by a flour sack, you were dead, as it were. There were different rules as to what being "dead" meant within the context of the game. Most of these games were either capture-the-flag or foxes-and-hounds variations. But instead of tag or tackle, it was being hit by a flour sack.

Needless to say, this was incredibly fun—and most of the time we played the games at night. And the place that we went on for most of our combat campouts was Daniel land, the eighty acres in Randolph County, where Emmett and Myrtice had once built their weekend cabin—the cabin that was robbed and burned. We also did several campouts on my grandfather's portion of land that he inherited from George Francis Daniel, the "forty acres," as we called it, where he had his hobby farm in Randolph County.

We used the dirt road that ran through the middle of the eighty acres, running up and down it, fighting with flour sacks. I always tried to structure the games into some kind of narrative. Once we did an Old West version of the game. My father got some lead bars and put them in a crate. It was very heavy, and required two boys to carry. We spray-painted the lead a yellow color, and said that it was gold.

On that campout, we took over an old house that was falling down near the eighty acres one night. Roger, the other leadership corps boys, and I remade it into a saloon out of the Old West. The guys on the campout were supposed to wear either cowboy or Indian costumes of some sort, and they all played along pretty well. In the saloon we served root beer and snacks.

We had the Indian team raid the saloon and steal the gold. And then the cowboys had to go after them and try to re-capture the gold, if they could.

It was enormously fun chasing each other around up and down the dirt road and through the woods. On another one of these combat campouts, we had a "medieval knights" theme. We divided up into two armies. Before the campout, we all made shields from cardboard, and brought them out. This was another one that I orchestrated.

The knights fought on the forty acres. There was an area with a dip between two hills in the pasture there. So we put an army on one hill and the other one on the next hill over, across a small gulley, and had each of them build a fort. Then each army tried to capture the flag from the other fort, and take it back to their fort. Whoever was able to do this would win. We had various rules about what it meant when a knight got hit by a flour sack. You weren't dead eternally, but only for a certain amount of time, to keep it fun for the guys.

The first of these combat campouts we held at Pelham Range out at Fort McClellan. The Army was always eager to cooperate with Boy Scout troops because they figured it was a good recruiting tool, I suppose. So we often went to Pelham Range for campouts, when we had no other plans. It was an old training ground and range the Army seldom used anymore, but there were all sorts of quite dangerous things still lying about, such as unspent shells, and a great many tripwires in the woods that set off noisemakers. It wasn't hugely dangerous, or we wouldn't been allowed out there, but there was an element of peril, which I enjoyed. In fact, one night when I was sitting by the campfire telling a story during one of our evening gatherings, an unshot shell went off inside the campfire. Most of the maneuvers the Army did at Pelham Range were with blank ammunition. I think this one was a blank, but it may not have been. Anyway, it scared the bejesus out of all of us, and it happened at the climax of the story.

My father was in his element as Scoutmaster, and I wish he could've done it for the rest of his life. After I turned sixteen and got my car, I began to fall away from Scouts, and I think this disappointed and confused him. He wasn't great at handling my teenage self.

My brother was never into Scouts quite as much as I was, although he did participate a lot. My father had thrown himself into it, and then David and I sort of disappeared after a few years, leaving him with no real reason to continue, except for his own enjoyment. He did continue. He became an adult leader out in Dallas, for many years working with an inner-city troop. There are a lot of men who were once boys in Troop 9 who remember my dad as their Scoutmaster. I've heard from several of them over the years, and they all talk about how they were greatly affected by him, and the example he set, and the opportunities he gave them as youngsters to get out and do cool and interesting things.

The biggest activity in Boy Scouts at the time was going to the Philmont Scout Ranch in Cimarron, New Mexico. This is an enormous stretch of land that the Boy Scouts owned, given to them by an oil magnate. Philmont was sort of like Boy Scout Disney World. You would go on backpacking itineraries that took ten to twelve days. You would camp the whole time, and backpack from camping spot to camping spot. These camps were staffed by college-age guys who pretended to be miners or loggers or cowboys. Sometimes it wasn't a themed camp, and the staff did some other activity, such as rock climbing.

So each day, or at least every couple of days, we would hike from one camp to the next, and do an activity like climbing poles in the manner of old time loggers, or we'd go into an old mine that they had shored up for touring, with the older staff guys pretending to be Old West miners. It was incredibly fun.

My dad ultimately went to Philmont five times. The first time was with me, when I was fourteen, in 1977. This was the first time that I had ever climbed a high mountain. We rose before dawn one day, and went up Mount Baldy, the highest point there on the Scout ranch. We made it to the top in time to watch the sunrise.

This was one of the formative experiences of my life.

I remember the night before my dad had given me his wristwatch, which was one of those digital watches from the '70s with the LED readouts. He was pretty happy with that watch. Unfortunately, I accidentally broke the watchband. I always felt bad about that afterward, because I could've set it out beside my sleeping bag, but I was afraid that I wouldn't hear the little beeping alarm set to get us up before sunrise and make the hike, so I put it inside the sleeping bag— and proceeded to roll over on it during the night, breaking the band where it attached to the portion that held the watch.

One of my most intense memories from our first Philmont expedition was waking up in the middle of the night at a campground where, I believe, we had been engaged in gold panning activities the day before.

We were exhausted, and had not put our bear bag up very well in the tree that evening after dinner. What was more, we foolishly put it directly above where the tents were. These are classic mistakes for putting up a bear bag, by the way. A bear bag is where you put all your consumables for the night to keep them away from bears and other varmints.

I woke up late that night with the sound of my father's voice calling me.

"Tony, Tony," he said, "Get up!"

I sat up looked out through the tent flap.

"Look at the light," he said.

I did look at the light. He was shining a flashlight at my tent.

"Come toward the light," my father said. "I want you to come toward the light, slowly and straight to me."

I shoved on my boots, and did what he said. I moved toward the light, and soon was standing by him and several of the other scouts. I turned around and looked where he was still shining the flashlight. There were two bears. They had taken our bear bag out of the tree and torn it to pieces on the ground beside two tents, one of which was mine. They were eating all of our food. It's quite possible my father had saved my life.

Once we had everyone collected, we hiked away from that place as fast as we could. We went to the staff cabin, where they put us up for the night. They also resupplied us with food the next day. After that, we were very careful to put the bear bag far away from us—and very, very high.

It's a lesson I've applied to this day, and taught my kids.

On that trip we also went to a Mexican restaurant in Taos, and had some transcendent food. I grew to love Taos, and went back many times over the years. I even considered moving there at one point.

In Fort Worth, we had amazing steaks in the restaurant at the Fort Worth Stockyards. In the 1970s, it was not so much of a tourist attraction as a working area where stockmen came to buy and sell cattle. That steak was probably the best piece of meat I've ever had in my life. My father arranged all of this, looked into things, found this or that special activity. I may not have fully appreciated it then, but I appreciate it now.

We did have some major father-son contention on my second trip to Philmont. I was older. I went with the group when my brother and Jerry went out. It was 1984. I was twenty. I was not feeling like taking orders from anyone at the time. That was not a good trip. Dad and I argued almost the whole time, and I ended up leaving early.

He went back three more times after that. The next time that I went to Philmont was when I was in St. Louis at graduate school. This was 1987 or so. I was working with the Boy Scout Troop near where I lived. I had worked at summer camp that summer as Scoutcraft Director, and the St. Louis area council Philmont leaders had unexpectedly dropped out of the planned trip. The council sent me and a friend of mine from summer camp as the adult leaders, to take the boys out on the council-organized trip to Philmont. And I happened to be out there when my father was doing one of his Philmont trips with some of the Dallas boys that he had been working with.

We arranged beforehand to meet up, when we were both camping in different campgrounds, but both just below Mount Baldy. I hiked over in a rainstorm to find him. He had made a sign of cardboard that he'd tacked to a trail sign along the path. It was specifically written to me, and it detailed where he was camped, and provided a nicely drawn little map to get there, of course. I followed that, and we got together for a couple hours. I still have the sign in my memorabilia.

Then I went back to my group, and we both went to our separate homes. We didn't see each other again for at least a couple months.

My father was involved with the Boy Scout "secret organization," the Order of the Arrow, as well. He was made a Vigil member of that group, a high honor. He had this great red wool coat which was one of the official coats of the Boy Scouts. A lot of guys would sew the Order of the Arrow's round medallion patch on the back of these coats. But my father took it one step farther. He got the idea that he wanted to *embroider* a large-scale copy of the medallion on the back of his jacket. So he did. He proceeded to draw out the design on tracing paper, enlarge it, and sub tack it to the coat.

Using yarn and thread, he then embroidered an amazing Indian head on the back of the red scouting jacket. He wore this for years, and became known for it. The embroidery even had a little white cottony-wool feather analog trailing off from the headdress. It swung back and forth as he walked. This was one of the coolest jackets I've ever seen. I wish I still had it, but it disappeared somewhere along the way.

Jerry also finished the Wood Badge training, a big adult leader accomplishment. My father made many friends through the Boy Scouts. He was well-known and well-liked by the local council staff, particularly by a guy named Bob Hudson, who was the class of the local Scouting professionals. All in all, my father was his best self when he was involved with Scouting. It's too bad the organization was never really worthy of him.

Beyond Scouting, Dad and I climbed quite a few 14ers in Colorado over the years. The first one we went up was the highest point in Colorado, which is Mount Elbert, near Leadville, Colorado. Or I should say, he did not climb it, but I did. This was during my college years, I think. He, David, and I drove out to Colorado for a whirlwind three-day weekend. I had already driven out from Alabama. We drove from Dallas to Colorado in one day, and camped on the side of Elbert in the stand of aspen trees that marks the beginning of the southern trail.

We slept about four hours, then got up to make the climb. We started at a reasonably early hour and made some pretty good progress at first, but then the altitude kicked in. We were not acclimated. Usually altitude sickness hits me very hard for the first day that I'm at altitude. This time it did hit me in a most overwhelming way, but later. My father and David decided to stop at the tree line—that is, where the trees give out and the alpine tundra environment begins on mountains that high. I continued up.

By the time I got to the top, it was early afternoon. You don't want to be on a Colorado mountain peak after noon because that's when the storms come in. And a storm certainly came in on Elbert that day. I was not as prepared as I should've been. I was wearing a cotton shirt, for instance, which I knew even at that time was a big no-no. I also didn't have any rain gear with me.

A kindly climber loaned me his disposable poncho, so I was able to cover up from the rain. I hurried down with lightning crashing behind me, and met Dad and David at the tree line. At that point, I don't remember much, because I basically collapsed when we arrived back at the truck. We all drove into Leadville and found a hotel. That evening I wasn't sure if I was going to live to see the next day. I'm very glad that, despite the fact that we were all characteristically short on funds, my dad decided not to camp, but to get us a place to stay. We also ate a big meal, which I needed just as badly.

And then we headed back home the next day—directly into a major Texas thunderstorm (unrelated to the mountain weather). We were driving along somewhere between Dalhart and Amarillo, and lightning was hitting on either side of us, striking power poles within fifty or sixty feet of us, blowing up at least two transformers I witnessed. It was quite intense. My father drove. I finished up reading a novel by Barbara Pym.

Jerry later climbed Elbert a couple of times. He and I climbed Mount Massive together, which is nearby. I don't think we ever climbed Elbert together, however. But we did go out and climb many more 14ers. I think he and I climbed maybe fifteen to twenty together. I have climbed over thirty, at the moment. He also climbed several by himself over the years. He and I did the Chicago Basin in southern Colorado, those three peaks. The most intense was Mount Aeolus, which we climbed together in a sleet storm. Coming down was perilous, because you went from one little ledge to another, and, if you happened to slip, you could fall off the whole dang mountain in one fell swoop. But we made it down, and it was exhilarating.

Climbing Wyndham Peak with him was also interesting because it was my second time on that one, and I could lead.

We went so many other places together as well. We made trips to Big Bend National Park. We made trips to Guadalupe Peak in southwestern Texas. We went out to Palo Duro Canyon near Amarillo Texas. We went to Arches National Park more than once. The week before my wedding to Rika (which took place at her mother's place near Barcelona), he and I spent several days in the Jungfrau-Eiger Valley in Switzerland. We also went on a remarkable trip to Wyoming to the Wind River Range.

Our greatest, most epic trip ever was our climb of Mount Rainier in Washington State. I had been living out in Seattle for several years, and I had taken courses with a group called the Mountaineers. They taught me how to climb on glaciers and go up mountains like Rainier. I'd attempted Rainier before with another group, and we had been driven off by a storm. I'd also climbed several other peaks around the Cascades, and on the Olympic Peninsula, before Dad and I attempted Rainier. So I was fairly confident about getting up, but I knew it was going to be a monster.

My father drove out, and I trained him for a couple of days in rescue techniques. He picked them up quickly. We went over them using trees behind the bus where I was living on Vashon Island.

We decided to do the most common route, which is to go up to Camp Muir for the first night, and then climb the mountain on the second day. Muir is basically a rocky outcropping with a couple of huts and latrines on it at the top of the Muir Snowfield, maybe a third of the way up.

So we climbed up the Muir Snowfield, postholing our way. And that night we camped at Muir. Then problems set in. A storm system came up, and it hit intensely. There was no way to go up or down the next day. In fact, the night before there had been such a whiteout condition that, when I went out to go to the bathroom, I almost got lost coming back. At Camp Muir, you stayed in a stone hut that had multiple bunks made out of sheets of plywood. There was no heat, but it was a lot better than sleeping in a tent in a storm like that.

The conditions were far too dangerous the next morning, so, as soon as possible—which was the day after—we hiked back down the snowfield. Even that was difficult, despite wearing our crampons. The icy sheet on top of the snow was not stable.

We came back up about a week later. We climbed up the familiar trail to Muir, and things looked great. The next day we started up before first light. In the beginning, we were walking along with a group that had come from California. It was led by a guy who put these climbs together every couple of years. There was also a guided tour by the official guide service that ran the hut on the opposite end of Muir. They chugged up as well.

But, strangely enough, everyone got to the top of the volcano and then did not go to the high point of the mountain. This seemed to me to completely miss the point of climbing a mountain. Rainier is a volcano, so there is a crater on top. Approaching on the Muir route, you have to go over the lip, then down in the crater bowl, then up the other side where the high point is found—the actual summit of Mount Rainier. The other two groups just went up to the top of the lip and called it a day. They headed back down.

My father and I were astounded by this. We kept going, of course. We walked across the crater and were rewarded by seeing fumaroles—which are places where steam is shooting out from the volcano below (Rainier is still an active volcano). These form gigantic plumes of ice where the steam condenses above the fumaroles. It is eerie and beautiful.

We climbed up to the highest point and made our pictures there. Then we started back, and worked our way down fairly easily after that. The most difficult part of the climb was the spot where the glacier met the rock of the mountain. There is a steep separation, and sometimes a crevasse, in such spots. That was a place you had to climb up using belay techniques in order to keep from falling in the event of a slip. I climbed this part and belayed my dad up. It was a little bit tricky finding this spot on the way down, too. We'd mark it with crossed bamboo staves that we'd brought along, however, so it wasn't impossible to locate, and we did.

We came off the entire mountain that day, and then I think we drove to a hotel and didn't try to make it back to my bus. We were exhausted, of course. The one thing that we did not do right was put on lip balm that had sunscreen. Instead we used Carmex, which had no sunscreen added at the time. This was a big mistake. Our lips sunburned intensely and, over the course of the next few days, swelled up immensely. We looked like a couple of monsters.

My dad had to go back to Dallas like that, and he said it took a while for his lips to go down. It certainly took a while for mine to do so. My girlfriend at the time was repulsed.

But we had climbed a glaciated peak, and come down to tell about it. I still have some of our equipment from that climb. This was in 1993, so my father did it when he was fifty-three years old. Quite an accomplishment.

I remember visiting my father at work when he was at the U.S. Geological Survey. I went there several times, no doubt with my mother. He was in a large room that had several drafting tables in it, with a bunch of guys sitting around in a square shape, facing inward. Once he became the boss of the drafting room, he had a separate desk a little bit away, and his own drafting table.

What I remember most was his cool supplies and tools. He had every kind of press-type you could imagine. He had all sorts of rulers that let him draw lines and curves or circles of various sorts and sizes. But the thing I remember most is his number two turquoise HB pencils. He always used them. He thought they were by far the best pencils for mapmaking. And the other thing he had was a very cool electric eraser. It was a large, handheld electric device with an eraser tip. You would press a rocker switch to turn it on. It was shiny black, with silver trim. And it tapered down to a point with the eraser on the end. You could use that thing to erase anything quickly. And you could use it to cut through paper by just holding it in place and erasing until the paper had a hole in it. Very fun to play with.

Another thing I remember about that building was the elevator. He was on the second or third floor, and you had to take the elevator up. Well, it was an old elevator, and it did not always work properly. Sometimes the door would open on the inside of the elevator, but the outside portion of the door would not open. This exposed a bunch of door gears and pulleys all made of metal that looked sort of like the door guts showing themselves. It was frightening to me when the door didn't open. I was afraid we would be stuck in the elevator. But usually, after a couple of tries, whatever gear needed to catch caught, and the door would open all the way, and we could leave our little box prison.

Of course, I visited my father at his office in Dallas many times. He had a large drafting table there as well, although he had shifted over to doing a lot of his work on a big computer screen by the end of his time there. After working in the First National Bank building for years, Hunt moved, and he worked in this huge skyscraper in downtown Dallas that had been designed by the architect I. M. Pei. It was called Fountain Place, and was sixty stories high, the fifth highest building in Dallas at the time. It went up into a point, and had sort of a twisted mien to it. Several times he took us up to the very top of the building where there was a board room and conference and meeting area. We would go up at night and gaze out over the entire Dallas cityscape.

It was very cool.

While he was living in the suburb of Garland, he often took the bus to work instead of driving downtown. Once they moved to the southern suburb of DeSoto, he started driving in and parking more often. I think it was on those bus trips that he began planning the art and pottery that would occupy him in later years. I know he did a great deal of reading on the bus, as well.

They lived at first in Richardson, Texas, in an apartment, for a couple of years when they first moved out to Dallas. Then they moved to a smaller house in Garland, 6506 Alta Oaks, which they kept ownership of for the rest of the time that they lived in Dallas. But they wanted a larger house. So when a geologist at work told my dad that he was going to walk away from his mortgage, they moved down to his house in DeSoto, at 600 N Chattey Road, and kept up the payment on it, without actually buying and owning the place. My parents could sometimes make disastrous financial moves seem inevitable.

Anyway, they lived there for quite a few years. Finally, the real owner said he wanted to go ahead and sell the house, and have nothing more to do with it. So they moved back to the Garland house for their final years in Dallas. Within maybe a week or two from the time that they moved from the Desoto house, a huge tornado came through and razed that house to the ground.

It is utterly gone today, destroyed by the tornado, and a completely different house stands in its place. If my parents had stayed there another month, another week, everything they had, and possibly they themselves, would've been destroyed, as well.

My father's boss for many years at Hunt Oil was a fellow named

Ray Fairchild. Ray was the head of the international exploration division, and had made a name for himself by finding oil in politically unstable countries (or wannabe countries). Hunt would go in and take a chance on a place where the regime in power was in a shaky situation. Sometimes they lost out, but when they did not, they were often the only concessioner in the place, and could make a lot of money.

They did this in Yemen, especially. My father spent many years working on maps for South Yemen for the geologists and geophysicists looking for oil there. He also began to make graphic presentations for people in the company. I think that his reputation spread around the company for making really pretty slides.

In the end, he was put to use by the company president, Ray Hunt, on some presentations. Hunt liked my dad, and I think viewed him as a kind of house servant. My father encouraged this, because whenever anyone in the company needed couriering services—that is, taking material like maps or contracts or something like that, to other countries—my father would volunteer. This allowed my dad to make several trips down to Central and South America, and to London. While he was overseas he took full advantage of the opportunity to do some sightseeing, usually with a geologist colleague he'd met there. He also hosted a lot of foreign nationals who came to visit the Hunt headquarters in Dallas, especially Middle Easterners. He took them on trips Out West occasionally.

I think the company really appreciated him as a sort of ambassador, and his knowledge of places to go in Texas and beyond was invaluable to them. Plus, my dad had a lot of fun doing this. The one place he never got to, however, was the country he did so much work on, Yemen.

After about ten years, my father's beloved boss Ray Fairchild, retired. Fairchild himself soon developed Alzheimer's, and died of it some years later. Working for Fairchild was always the apex of my father's enjoyment of his job at Hunt Oil. Fairchild trusted and used Jerry's talents well.

After Fairchild was gone, my dad was shuffled around. At one point, he was made head of the cartography department. But he absolutely hated giving job reviews to the other cartographers. He really didn't want to be anyone's boss. Jerry was just not made for management. That was what it came down to, and he asked to be reassigned.

During his later years at Hunt, he began to take classes in the art departments of Dallas area community colleges. He had always done country crafts, mostly things that he had discovered in the famous Foxfire books, or remembered from his youth in Newell. He became an expert at making baskets out of oak slats, for instance. He also made baskets out of copper wire, beautiful fruit baskets, by weaving strands of stripped wire together. But what he really enjoyed most, at that time, was throwing pots.

Jerry made himself into an expert potter, but that was not enough. He was far more interested in the art of ceramics. As always, he was an artist-craftsman, not a craftsman alone. He was fascinated by the old way of doing things.

In fact, he went to the famous artisanal school of Penland, in North Carolina near Asheville, for a week of instruction. There he worked on his pottery with expert teachers and mentors.

When there was an old fashioned way of doing woodwork, pottery, or anything else, he'd study and adapt it. Jerry made himself a pottery kickwheel, a foot-powered concrete flywheel like the old-time potters used (well, theirs were likely made of stone). He began to exclusively throw pots on this man-powered kickwheel. In fact, he and some of his potter friends brought the very heavy device to craft fairs and demonstrations in parks around Dallas, where Jerry took part in putting on shows, throwing pots, and helping people learn how to do it themselves. He became very good at using that kickwheel, I can tell you. It isn't that easy. And the thing didn't require any electric power, whatsoever.

From pottery, Jerry expanded into metalwork. I'm not sure how he got interested in welding, but he started putting together larger and larger metallic sculptures. They greatly resembled the work of Alexander Calder, the great American sculptor, best known for his mobiles. My father adored Calder's work, especially the larger sculptures, and we went to see examples of these in Toronto once on a long drive up from New York, where I lived at the time. He visited me twice in New York, and on one trip we rode bicycles around Manhattan, took the skyway over to Roosevelt Island, and then circled back into Manhattan over the Triborough Bridge. It was an epic ride we made that day.

By the time he retired in 2004, he wanted to devote his time to making more pottery and creating the large metallic sculptures that fascinated him. In the late 1990s, he'd undertaken a commission for a nuclear scientist and made a depiction of an amazing atom being smashed inside a particle accelerator. It was about six feet high and made of painted metallic strips. He showed some of his work in galleries around Dallas, and had a large piece sitting on a community campus for many years.

But his retirement of sculpting and pottery creation was not to be. By the time he had gotten the barn built and the dogs transferred to Centerville, his Alzheimer's had kicked in. He was unable to complete any large metal works after he moved there. There were incomplete pieces lying around the land there for several years. All of the sculptures he'd done that were really good he did before he retired.

Jerry was about five-foot-ten-inches in height. He had brown hair and a medium build. He had a fair complexion and sunburned easily. In later years, he had a bout of skin cancer—a more virulent sort, that had to be surgically scraped from his chest. He suffered from a case of shingles not long after that.

During the 1970s, he let himself get a little chubby. By the 1980s, he had lost that weight, and remained skinny and fit for the rest of his life. During the 70s, he sported a mustache for several years, but cut it off after they were no longer fashionable. During his twenties and early thirties, he wore fashionable clothes and dressed in a very iconic 70s manner, which I believe was due to my mother's influence.

After he got to Anniston, he started dressing fairly countrified. But the one thing was always constant. He wore a collared shirt, a collared shirt that he tucked in, especially on work sites. This single item of clothing was the big sartorial differentiator between the hired help and the contractors on commercial jobsites in the South.

He was very careful to keep up appearances wherever he was, that's for sure. While at Hunt Oil, he had to wear a suit every day. He came to greatly dislike those suits, and that played into his final will, which I will tell you about soon. He had blue eyes, intense, light-blue eyes. He had 20/20 vision his entire life, probably better than 20/20 for most of it. He was proud of his eyesight. This is one of the reasons he thought about being a pilot when he was younger.

He fell off a ladder and broke a toe in 2010. A surgeon had to sever the tendon in that toe. Other than that, I don't think he ever had any bodily injury—well, aside from being burned when he was nine. He wasn't sick much when he was younger. I remember his having the flu once or twice, and being miserable with that, but not much else. In his fifties, he developed the skin cancer that had to be dealt with. He also had that particularly uncomfortable case of shingles in the same decade. He suffered from type II diabetes when he was in his early 60s, as well. He was driving along the interstate in Dallas one night, and suddenly couldn't see. He just went blind. This was due to the diabetes, and was soon corrected by proper diet.

He had some pretty thick cataracts removed. Yet, most of his life, he was hardy and hale, and this lasted to the point where he needed heart surgery. Even after that, he was tough and strong still. If the Alzheimer's hadn't gotten him, I think he would've been a strong old man for many years, and would probably still be around going hiking with me, maybe even surging up a few mountains ahead of me. I would have liked that. I know he would have.

My father created a will which has become somewhat legendary among my friends and my family. In it, he detailed what he wanted done when he died. He figured he had to be displayed in some manner for my mother's sake, or he would probably rather have gone on to cremation immediately. At his funeral service, he wanted to be shown in a soft, button-down shirt, no suit or tie. He wanted no preachers, no crying. He wanted no flowers. He wanted some photos he'd made of flowers to be shown, if necessary.

He wanted to be wearing jeans. Not Levis or Lee jeans, but to be wearing Wrangler jeans, his favorite brand. He had several other requests as well. But the main thing was, he wanted to be cremated— and to have his remains divided into twenty-five sacks.

Twenty-five penny-candy sacks, he called them. These were to be placed into two green ammunition boxes, the kind you can get from army surplus stores. And then he had twenty-five different places that he wanted these ashes scattered. I was supposed to take one box and my brother David the other. He lists very specifically where these places are in the will-like document that I have.

I knew about this thing for years, and had a copy of it in my files. He wrote it when he was fifty, so there are parts of it that were fairly out of date. But after he died, I got it out, and we tried to do it almost down to the letter. I had them embalm him, even though he was going to be cremated, so that we could have a final showing. His brother and sister, Ricky and Patricia, came up for the funeral service. I delivered the eulogy, which I will include here. And then I sent him away to be cremated.

And as of now, I am making plans to distribute the ashes in the many places that he wished them to be placed. It will probably take several years to accomplish. My wife and children will help me with it. Mostly the locations are national parks or other beautiful spots. Each has something specific about it that he recounts in the will, and several requests have quirky qualifiers, as well.

It's a wonderful document, and we will try to honor it the way he wanted. In the meantime, there he sits in the ammunition box I bought to place his ashes in. He is on the shelf in the cabinet here in my study, or at least his ashes are. He and I will soon be going on our last journeys together. I know that they, too, will be amazing.

Here's the eulogy I wrote and delivered at Jerry's funeral.

Jerry A. Daniel Eulogy

⋆⊱═◉═⊰⋆

Delivered at His Funeral, 2019 10 29

If you want to know the outlines of my father's life, you can read about it in his obituary. That, of course, barely scratches the surface. The things he did were so varied, his creative spirit was so profligate, I could spend hours here recounting it. In 2007, when he knew he was at the beginning stage of his Alzheimer's Disease, he and I sat down and did something like that with a tape recorder. Even that recording session was only touching on moments, moments that he considered unique or memorable to him. I have all those recordings still, and have been listening to them today. Of course, I'll make them available for anyone who wants to hear them. Daddy left a beautiful legacy in these for his family, his children and grandchildren, and for his descendants beyond that. They are great.

Now, though, I'd like to say something about not what

Daddy did necessarily, but what Daddy was *like*. What was the spirit and character of Jerry A. Daniel, my father?

As my children know, if they asked their Opa Bu his favorite color, he would pause for a moment, smile slightly, and then say—what?

Sky-blue pink.

He would leave them—and now you—to figure out what he meant by that. But for those who have seen the photographs he took, the drawings he made, and the sculptures he created, you will see that color there, worked into the materials one way or another. Sky-blue pink.

Daddy was an artist in the truest sense of the word. The world affected him, and he tried to communicate what he experienced in drawings, photography, painting, pottery, and sculpture. He began as a draftsman, because that was what a boy with artistic ability did growing up in Anniston in the 1940s and 50s. As we in the family know, my grandparents wanted him to be an electrical engineer, but he never had the temperament for that. He's was not an analyst primarily, although he had great analytic skill. He was an interpreter. A synthesizer.

So he became a mapmaker instead, and made his living for many years doing that job first at the U.S. Geological Survey in Tuscaloosa Alabama, and doing side jobs for the state geologist, then eventually as a cartographer, at times the chief cartographer, at Hunt Oil in Dallas, Texas. The ability to picture the three dimensional nature of the world in his mind came as naturally to him as breathing. This was how his memory worked, as well.

In these several hours of recordings I've been listening to, I came across this fact again and again. These recordings aren't really stories, although they contain some good stories. But Daddy was not a storyteller, not in the conventional sense. He admired storytellers. He loved greatly his father-in-law, Coker Montgomery, who was a consummate teller of tales. Daddy didn't cry a lot, hardly ever, but he would tear up when talking about Coker after my grandfather died. Daddy always called him Mr. Montgomery.

Daddy was no slouch when it came to words himself, but his true talent lay elsewhere. His memories occurred as vignettes, as pictures, that stuck with him over the years. Pictures. Images. Geometry. Lines. Color. That was the way Daddy's mind worked.

The one thing that struck me the most listening to these recordings, is Daddy's deep sense of place, of setting. This always came first in his recollection of things. He recalls the landscape, the weather and the sky, the nearby landmarks—and that is his way into remembering the people and the story or moment he wants to recount.

Blue Mountain in Anniston. He spent a large part of his boyhood climbing around on it in all sorts of weather. He went with his friends to hunt flying squirrels with BB guns there. To climb the fire watchtower, which looked out of the other side and into the firing ranges and training ground of the Army's Fort McClellan, which was adjacent to the town. He recalls smoke and mortar fire. He remembers weekend days going to the John B. LeGarde Sand Pit on the other side of Anniston, and climbing the conveyor belts, and jumping off the end to land many feet below in the sand piles.

Blue Mountain. Cheaha Mountain, which he loved. All the mountains surrounding his Northeast Alabama home. These framed his early memories. Then his world broadened as he married, traveled, and eventually moved far away to Texas, where he would spend his last thirty years. And from there the American West, where he would spend decades traveling about, climbing mountains, traveling through canyons, deserts, mesas, and badlands, before coming to stay with us here in his final years.

Landscape and weather, geology, geography, meteorology, were Daddy's main mode of seeing the world. But a second was his fascination with clever ideas and devices. He loved neat ideas that were twists on old ways of doing things. His favorite method for building an outdoor fire, for instance, was the Dakota hole, which he learned from his friend Maran Coleburn, the deaf scoutmaster of the deaf Boy Scout troop from Talladega School for the Deaf. When he first met Maran,

Daddy was far more fascinated by the fire Maran was using than with his deafness, which Daddy just accepted, as was usual with him. But a Dakota hole—now that was fascinating to Daddy.

A Dakota hole is two post holes dug about four inches apart and a couple of feet deep. These are connected at the bottom by a tunnel. You build a fire on one side with little sticks, squaw wood, we used to call it, and the other side serves as a chimney. It is perfect for a small cooking fire, and it can never be put out by wind. For years after Daddy learned how to make them, we built Dakota holes on Scout campouts, in the Smokies, the Great Plains, and anywhere else he could get them to work.

Daddy loved a good idea, a twist on an accepted way of doing things, and he was constantly thinking of ways to apply old ideas in new ways. As I said, he was good at analysis, but his true passion, his true heart and talent, was as a synthesizer, a maker, a creator, who worked with the past to remake the present, to bring what had gone before back to life in an interesting, useful way. This was the opposite of nostalgia, but somehow always respectful, never a rejection of what had gone before.

For example, I remember using Dakota holes to cook breakfast at a Boy Scout expo in Anniston one weekend. Daddy was the Scoutmaster of my and David's troop for many years. Anyways, he took a strong flat rock, put it on tent stakes, spread some oil on top and we scouts cooked pounds of sausage, which we then gave out to the passing crowd on sample plates. People were fascinated by the process, and appreciated the sausage, too.

Once, in his Tuscaloosa days, he discovered a tattered old map of Alabama from 1823 in the archives at the University of Alabama and got another idea. He remade that map using his cartographic skills. You can see it right here. He had this printed on parchment paper, and would later decoupage Alabama 1823 maps onto old pieces of wood he'd cut, routered, and stained, or sometimes on the wooden shingles of the old country houses that he mined for his map wood. We spent a considerable part of my earlier childhood going to craft fairs and selling these creations to folks. He loved to talk to people about them, and if he enjoyed the conversation, he would often let his customers name their own price, just so they walked away with something he believed they truly would appreciate.

In so many ways, Daddy was of the world, not against it. He was the opposite of an alienated artist. He was a part of everything and everyone around him, and he felt it and it flowed through him. He didn't try to stand out as a character. He let his talent, his way of living, do the talking. In fact, when I was younger I sometimes wondered if he was even a conscious person at all. He seemed like a conduit of nature to me. Being around him was like looking through a stained glass window out upon creation.

He was the stained glass for me then. When I grew older, we talked more as men, and I understood he *was* a man like any other, with all the feelings and foibles, shortcomings and strengths, of a man. But I still have that sense of Daddy as a window that didn't change what you were seeing, but somehow made reality deeper and richer when you were viewing it with him, through him. He deeply loved actual stained glass, by the way, and sometimes worked with it. For many years, we had, hanging over the kitchen table, this great Tiffany-style lamp he made.

He married my mother when he was twenty and she was nineteen. He met her at a Civil Air Patrol mixer at Maxwell Air Force Base in Montgomery, Alabama. This is a family legend now. Once, when I was very young, I made Mom a Tinkertoy bracelet that was "like" the one I imagined her wearing at that little get together.

They were married for fifty-nine years. I came along in the married student trailer park at the University of Alabama (well, actually I was born at Druid City Hospital, as was my brother, David). My parents were, and are, a unit. They were loving and argumentative, and then always loving again. It was sometimes bewildering growing up, but I felt deeply secure in the nest of my family. It was beyond just romantic love, or even respect. They are pair bonded, like swans or eagles. My mother was and is, in many ways, my father's voice in the world. She could articulate what he sometimes could not. She also pushed him on his art, to do what he loved, to be ambitious about expressing what was in his soul and his vision. He would never have done the things he did, or gone the places he went, without her to urge him onward.

In the end it was the form of the world that moved my father most of all, the curve of the rock in canyons, the spread of broken granite on the mountain tops he climbed, the swirls and curls of clouds at sunset and sunrise. He loved to make sunset and sunrise photos. He also loved the shapes of flowers, and made hundreds of pictures of them. In later years, he incorporated that shape, that natural flow of form and matter, into his sculptures. He never ran out of ideas. I still have his notebooks, full of sculpture, and pottery, and art ideas. He saw into the deep structure of nature, not as a scientist or even as a lover of nature, but as an artist, as a sub-creator, an apprentice to creator of Heaven and Earth.

And that is what I hope and believe he is doing now. I believe he has completed his apprenticeship here on Earth, and the Lord has taken him away to do important work in some reality that is more deep and wide than any we can imagine. Daddy caught a glimpse of that greater reality when he was among us, I think. He sought all his life to communicate what he was seeing.

Now he is God's journeyman, I believe in my heart. He has joined in the eternal work, the real work, he was born to accomplish, the ornamentation of the universe itself with beauty. I believe he is working as an artist still, right now, as God's draftsman, His cartographer, His potter and sculptor, to help bring splendor and color and form and life to all manner of places and things and actualities beyond our present comprehension. But even there, in that place beyond time, that eternal present where all things take their being, I think matters won't have changed so much that he won't be able to pull out his favorite color and paint with it in new and wondrous ways. In ways inconceivable, but also in ways that I believe we can and will see occasionally, if we look up.

When we look up—and out. Beyond the clouds. Beyond the mountains and river and houses and schools and churches and cars and pets and children. But also within all of that. All of them. Within all these things. We can glimpse the inner glow of everyday reality that Daddy was made by his Creator to see. To comprehend. And to work with. It's in the rocks, the shapes, the forms, the colors of all the world. Sky-blue pink. That is my father's favorite color.

⋯⊷━⊶⋯

The Kite

One of the most enduring memories of my childhood, and yet one of the most elusive, is of flying a kite with my father and my brother at a school playground one day. I think it was at the Golden Springs Elementary School playground in Anniston. But, then again, I might have been younger, and it may have been the Skyland Park playground in Tuscaloosa. Deduction tells me that it was probably in Anniston, but I can't recall.

Jerry built a kite. I think it was in March, and there was some sort of kite flying contest we were competing in. It was a paper kite, one of the standard-shaped varieties. Now my father knew a lot about paper airplanes and kites. He had experimented as an adult, I'm sure. He'd certainly made some killer paper airplanes with the glossy map paper from his work. He had flown a lot of kites as a kid. He knew what to do.

The main thing you need after you get a kite in the air is a sturdy anchor in the sky, a great tail. My father made an amazing tail for that kite. We took every old sheet we could find at home, and he may have bought a couple more from the thrift store. We took those sheets and cut them into strips. And then we tied all these strips tightly together in a long, long train. It must've been a twenty or even thirty-foot tail. It was enormously long. There were others flying kites nearby, and they obviously didn't think we would get the thing off the ground.

It did take a while to get the kite up. My father and I worked at it, with David giving encouragement. But this was a very windy day, something my father had taken into account, and we did get it airborne. He slowly worked it up, and I made sure the tail didn't snag as it left the ground.

After that, it was a matter of hanging on—because that kite was going places. It went higher and higher. The tail trailing behind it made it quite visible to us, at least when it was relatively nearby. But then it started pulling out the twine. My father knew this was going to happen. He had acquired a bunch of twine from, I believe, the textile place in Anniston, Blue Mountain Industries. If not there, maybe it was contractor chord used for laying out foundations. I know for sure that it was exceptionally strong stuff.

At first, we attached this to a homemade spooling device, a stick with the spool tube on it. This lasted for about two spools. The critical moment you had to watch for was when a spool played out. He had to attach the end of a second spool to that one, and keep feeding line to the kite.

Into the third spool or so, the drag from the kite became too much for a boy—or even a man—to hold. Dad attached the spool to the bumper of our car. He rigged the spool to a piece of strong wire, so it could still play out.

And out it went, farther and farther. The kite kept pulling out twine, and after one spindle was done, Dad tied the ends together and started another, and then another. Soon the kite was a tiny speck, far away in the sky.

We watched it for what seemed like hours to me. People around us marveled. Finally, after Lord knows how many spools, we could no longer even *see* the kite, it was so far away. It may have gone over the curvature of the Earth. My father, who had the best eyesight of any human being I've ever met, claimed he *thought* he saw it. The only way we knew it was still there was because of the tension on the string. And the fact that it kept playing out.

Again, my memory is faulty. I know my father later counted up the spools and said that the kite was *three miles out*. But I also recalled him saying that he thought it was *seven miles* away.

In the late afternoon, the string finally broke.

We got in the car and followed that twine as far as we could, but it stretched for miles. Literally miles. We lost it in some woods.

I think my father estimated that he had reeled out three miles of twine, and that the winds had probably carried the kite seven miles away. We searched around in the car in what I think was a half-circle roughly seven miles in radius.

I don't know how Jerry knew to have that much twine available, but he did. He knew he was going to get that kite a long way up, and a long way away. It was the most amazing kite flight I've ever seen. I'll never forget looking far into the distance and catching the speck that was our kite still flying there, and Jerry Daniel, my dad, spooling it out, checking on his twine, and letting it spool out even farther.

We never found the kite. It had probably come down in a forest somewhere.

But sometimes I like to think maybe the kite just kept going, kept circling around over the horizon, around the Earth itself, and is still up there somewhere. My rational mind knows it must have crashed, but, at least in spirit, that kite we made is still flying. And it will be up there as long as there's a curve to the planet.

Appendix
Useful Genealogical Tables and Charts
❖❖❖ ❖❖❖

**Pedigree Chart for
Tony Daniel**

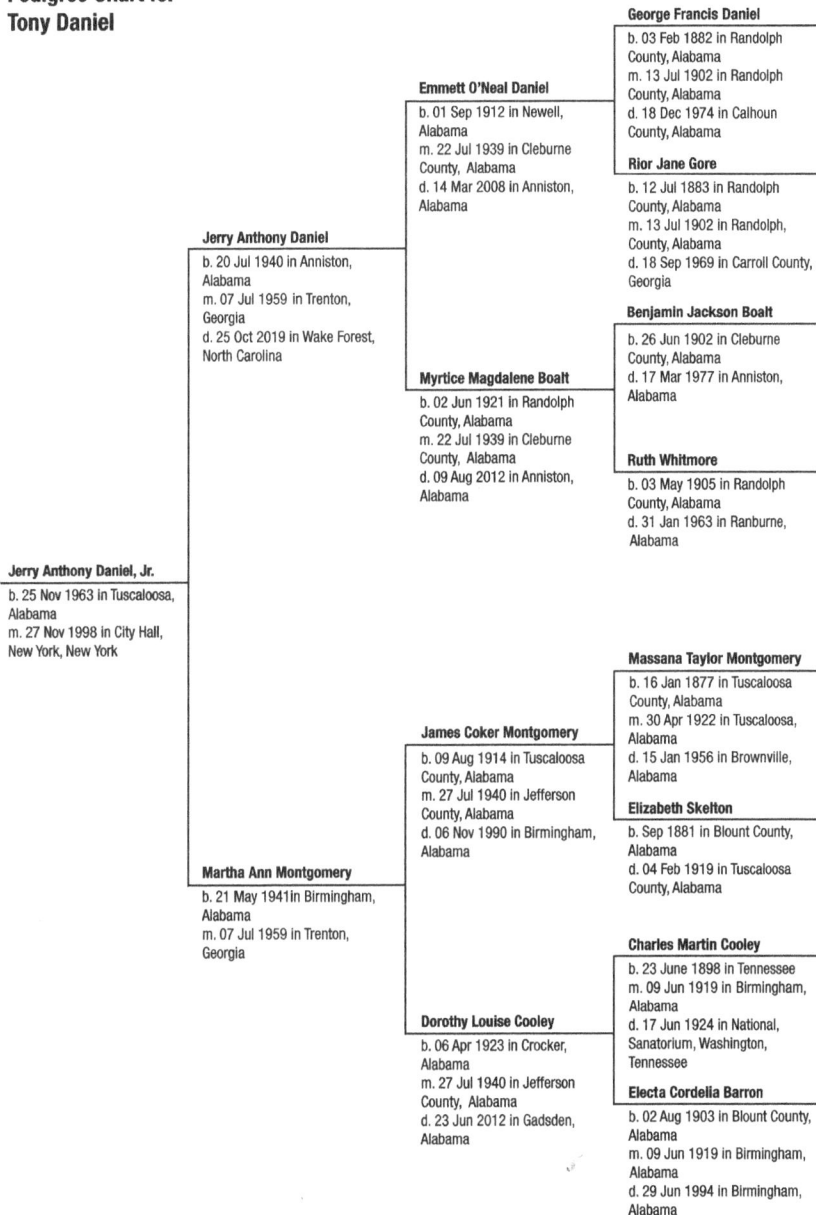

George Francis Daniel
b. 03 Feb 1882 in Randolph County, Alabama
m. 13 Jul 1902 in Randolph County, Alabama
d. 18 Dec 1974 in Calhoun County, Alabama

Emmett O'Neal Daniel
b. 01 Sep 1912 in Newell, Alabama
m. 22 Jul 1939 in Cleburne County, Alabama
d. 14 Mar 2008 in Anniston, Alabama

Rior Jane Gore
b. 12 Jul 1883 in Randolph County, Alabama
m. 13 Jul 1902 in Randolph, County, Alabama
d. 18 Sep 1969 in Carroll County, Georgia

Jerry Anthony Daniel
b. 20 Jul 1940 in Anniston, Alabama
m. 07 Jul 1959 in Trenton, Georgia
d. 25 Oct 2019 in Wake Forest, North Carolina

Benjamin Jackson Boalt
b. 26 Jun 1902 in Cleburne County, Alabama
d. 17 Mar 1977 in Anniston, Alabama

Myrtice Magdalene Boalt
b. 02 Jun 1921 in Randolph County, Alabama
m. 22 Jul 1939 in Cleburne County, Alabama
d. 09 Aug 2012 in Anniston, Alabama

Ruth Whitmore
b. 03 May 1905 in Randolph County, Alabama
d. 31 Jan 1963 in Ranburne, Alabama

Jerry Anthony Daniel, Jr.
b. 25 Nov 1963 in Tuscaloosa, Alabama
m. 27 Nov 1998 in City Hall, New York, New York

Massana Taylor Montgomery
b. 16 Jan 1877 in Tuscaloosa County, Alabama
m. 30 Apr 1922 in Tuscaloosa, Alabama
d. 15 Jan 1956 in Brownville, Alabama

James Coker Montgomery
b. 09 Aug 1914 in Tuscaloosa County, Alabama
m. 27 Jul 1940 in Jefferson County, Alabama
d. 06 Nov 1990 in Birmingham, Alabama

Elizabeth Skelton
b. Sep 1881 in Blount County, Alabama
d. 04 Feb 1919 in Tuscaloosa County, Alabama

Martha Ann Montgomery
b. 21 May 1941 in Birmingham, Alabama
m. 07 Jul 1959 in Trenton, Georgia

Charles Martin Cooley
b. 23 June 1898 in Tennessee
m. 09 Jun 1919 in Birmingham, Alabama
d. 17 Jun 1924 in National, Sanatorium, Washington, Tennessee

Dorothy Louise Cooley
b. 06 Apr 1923 in Crocker, Alabama
m. 27 Jul 1940 in Jefferson County, Alabama
d. 23 Jun 2012 in Gadsden, Alabama

Electa Cordelia Barron
b. 02 Aug 1903 in Blount County, Alabama
m. 09 Jun 1919 in Birmingham, Alabama
d. 29 Jun 1994 in Birmingham, Alabama

181

Daniel

Jerry Anthony Daniel, Sr.
b: 20 Jul 1940, in Anniston, Alabama
m: 07 Jul 1959, in Trenton, Georgia
d: 25 Oct 2019, in Wake Forest, North Carolina

Jerry Anthony Daniel, Sr. Parents
Emmett O'Neal Daniel
b: 01 Sep 1912 in Newell, Alabama
m: 22 Jul 1939 in Cleburne, Alabama
d: 14 Mar 2008 in Anniston, Alabama

Myrtice Magdalene Boalt
b: 02 Jun 1921 in Randolph County, Alabama
m: 22 Jul 1939 in Cleburne, Alabama
d: 09 Aug 2012 in Anniston, Alabama

Children of Emmett O'Neal and Myrtice Daniel
Jerry Anthony Daniel, Sr. (1940-2019)
Patricia Ann Daniel (born 1949; daughter: Cindy Dulaney)
Sandra Joyce Daniel (born 1950)
Ricky Carl Daniel (born 1951)

Emmett O'Neal Daniel's Parents
George Francis Daniel
b: 03 Feb 1882 in Randolph County, Alabama
m: 13 Jul 1902 in Randolph County, Alabama
d: 18 Dec 1974 in Calhoun County, Alabama

Rior Jane Gore
b: 12 Jul 1883 in Randolph County, Alabama
m: 13 Jul 1902 in Randolph, Alabama
d: 18 Sep 1969 in Carroll County, Georgia

George Francis Daniel's Parents
Isaac Elijah Daniel
b: 19 Dec 1858 in Lamar, Alabama
m: 1877
d: 09 Apr 1936 in Tallapoosa, Georgia

Susan Esther Dorrough
b: 11 Aug 1855 in Harris, Georgia
m: 1877
d: 05 Apr 1932 in Tallapoosa, Georgia

Isaac Elijah Daniel's Parents
Hartford Moss Daniel
b: 25 Oct 1839 in Newton, Georgia
m: 1856 in Alabama
d: 01 Jul 1915 in Graham, Alabama

Elizabeth J. Williams
b: 08 May 1842 in Bibb County, Alabama
m: 1856 in Alabama
d: 27 Feb 1917 in Newell, Alabama

Hartford Moss Daniel's Parents
Isaac Beck Daniel
b: 16 Apr 1814 in Tattnall, Georgia
m: 1834 in Newton, Georgia
d: Feb 1884 in Lamar, Alabama

Elizabeth Lovvorn
b: 16 Apr 1814 in Morgan, Georgia
m: 1834 in Newton, Georgia
d: 1880 in Lamar, Alabama

Montgomery

Tony Daniel's Mother
Martha Ann Montgomery
b: 21 May 1941in Birmingham, Alabama
m: 07 Jul 1959 in Trenton, Georgia

Martha Ann Montgomery's Father and Mother
James Coker Montgomery
b: 09 Aug 1914 in Tuscaloosa County, Alabama
m: 27 Jul 1940 in Jefferson County, Alabama
d: 06 Dec 1990 in Birmingham, Alabama

Dorothy Louise Cooley
b: 06 Apr 1923 in Crocker, Alabama
m: 27 Jul 1940 in Jefferson County, Alabama
d: 23 Jun 2012 in Gadsden, Alabama

Children of James Coker and Dorothy Louise Montgomery
Martha Ann Montgomery (b: 1941, mother of
Tony and David Daniel)
Janice Fay Montgomery (b: 1947, d: 2015, mother of
Christopher Scott England)

Coker Montgomery's Father and Mother
M. Taylor Montgomery
b: 16 Jan 1877 in Tuscaloosa County, Alabama
d: 15 Jan 1956 in Tuscaloosa County, Alabama

Elizabeth Skelton
b: Sep 1881 in Alabama
d: 04 Feb 1919 in Buhl, Alabama

M. Taylor Montgomery's Father and Mother
William Baines Montgomery
b: 06 May 1855 in Northport, Tuscaloosa, Alabama
m: 28 Mar 1876 in Tuscaloosa County, Alabama
d: 16 Sep 1916 in Tuscaloosa County, Alabama

Narcissus Arbella Loftis
b: 03 Jan 1856 in Alabama
m: 1876 in Alabama
d: 16 Apr 1941 in Coker, Alabama

Family of Tony and Rika Daniel

Spouse
Jerry Anthony Daniel, Jr.
b. 1963, Tuscaloosa, Alabama
m. 1998, New York, New York

Spouse
Rika Verena Weinem Daniel
b. 1970, Koenigstein, Hessen, Germany
m. 1998, New York, New York

Children
Coker Montgomery Daniel
b. 2003, New York, New York

Hans Hoffmann Daniel
b. 2006, Allen, Texas

About the Author

Tony Daniel was born in Tuscaloosa, Alabama. He grew up in Tuscaloosa and Anniston, Alabama, before attending college in Birmingham, Alabama. Daniel is the author of many science fiction novels and award-winning short stories. He was a Hugo finalist for his short story "Life on the Moon," which also won the Asimov's Reader's Choice Award. In the 1990s, he founded and directed the Automatic Vaudeville dramatic group in New York City. Then, during the early 2000s, he was a story editor and producer of audiodrama at SCIFI.COM's Seeing Ear Theatre. He coauthored screenplays for horror movies that have appeared on two cable channels. Daniel has also written many essays and reviews for venues as varied as *The Stranger* and *The Federalist*. During the mid-2000s, he moved to Texas and taught literature and writing for six years on both an undergraduate and graduate level at the University of Texas at Dallas. He is currently Senior Editor at Baen Books, which has editorial offices in North Carolina. Daniel attended Birmingham-Southern College, in Birmingham, Alabama, where he majored in philosophy. He got his Masters in English from Washington University in St. Louis. He also attended the University of Southern California CNTV graduate program in Los Angeles before moving to Seattle to begin a writing career. He lived in the Seattle area for five years, primarily on Vashon Island in an old city bus. Since then, he has lived in Prague, New York City, Randolph and Cherokee Counties in Alabama, Sant Llorenc Savall, near Barcelona, and Allen, Texas, near Dallas. He currently resides in Wake Forest, North Carolina, with his wife Rika, and children, Cokie and Hans.

www.ingramcontent.com/pod-product-compliance
Lightning Source LLC
LaVergne TN
LVHW011349080426
835511LV00005B/199